ROBERTO CLEMENTE: Batting King

Throughout his baseball career Roberto Clemente has been plagued with aches and pains. And throughout that same career he has plagued National League pitchers with his numerous and timely hits. When Clemente stroked his two thousandth major league hit in September, 1966, only eight other players then active in both the National and the American leagues had passed the 2,000-hit mark. The all-round baseball natural from Puerto Rico, Clemente can chase and catch a fly ball that the batter is sure will be a hit. He can throw men out on the bases when they are sure they can easily outrun Clemente's arm. And he himself can run, often scoring from first on a single.

ROBERTO CLEMENTE
Batting King

By Arnold Hano

G. P. PUTNAM'S SONS

NEW YORK

 Published simultaneously in the Dominion of Canada by Longmans Canada Limited, Toronto.

Library of Congress Catalog Card Number: 68-15049

PRINTED IN THE UNITED STATES OF AMERICA
10 up

Contents

Sports Shelf Biographies You Will Enjoy

Sandy Koufax: Strikeout King
By Arnold Hano

Willie Mays: Coast to Coast Giant
By Charles Einstein

Mickey Mantle: Mister Yankee
By Al Silverman

Ken Boyer
By David Lipman

Ted Williams
By Ray Robinson

Stan Musial: Baseball's Durable "Man"
By Ray Robinson

My Ups and Downs in Baseball
By Orlando Cepeda, with Charles Einstein

Roberto Clemente: Batting King
By Arnold Hano

1

"Did He Get Them All Off Us?"

Friday, September 2, 1966
Forbes Field
Fifth inning, Pittsburgh Pirates vs. Chicago Cubs

ON THE MOUND for Chicago towered a lanky youngster named Ferguson Jenkins, all six feet five inches of him. On the bases, two Pirate runners edged away to short prancing leads. And at bat crouched Roberto Clemente, his right foot rubbing out the chalk at the far end of the batter's box. The score was 1–0, Pittsburgh, but in September of a National League pennant race, one-run leads melt like ice cubes in the Puerto Rican sun.

And this son of Puerto Rico felt like melting. All his career, Roberto Clemente has been subjected to aches and pains and ills often enough and intense enough to fell an ox. Now he was tired, just plain fatigued.

Jenkins fired his fast ball, on the outside corner of the plate, and Clemente swung. The ball rose in a blur of white, and buried itself in the right-field seats. Three runs scored. The 1–0 game had been burst open. Pittsburgh went on to win, 7–3.

This was Roberto Clemente's 2,000th base hit. With it, he joined eight other active ballplayers. Their names are a thunder roll of greatness: Willie Mays, Hank Aaron, Al Kaline, Harvey Kuenn, Mickey Mantle, Ernie Banks, Ken Boyer, and Eddie Mathews. Only 115 men in all of baseball's history, from the dawn of the century when Barney Dreyfus began the first great Pittsburgh dynasty, had made 2,000 hits.

The home run was Roberto Clemente's twenty-third of the season, tying his previous career high. The three runs batted in boosted his total to 101, first time he'd ever hurdled the century mark.

But most important, with this 2,000th hit, and with the Pittsburgh win, the Pirates again led the National League by a slender single game. All through the summer of 1966, three teams had clawed at each other, the San Francisco Giants, with their two right-handed aces, Juan Marichal and Gaylord Perry, and the incomparable Willie Mays; the defending champion Los Angeles Dodgers, with Sandy Koufax, marvelous relief pitching, burning speed on the bases, and intense pride; and the Pittsburgh Pirates, picked by nobody to win the flag, a team without pitching depth and, indeed, without a pitching leader, but a team that chewed off runs with double plays and then clubbed you to death with its bats, a crew of line-drive sluggers not seen in Pittsburgh since the fabled seasons of Paul and Lloyd Waner, Kiki Cuyler, Arky Vaughan, and Pie Traynor.

At the head of this '66 Pirate team was its blazing right fielder, a man who had become in the decade of the 1960s the greatest hitter in baseball, batting king of his league in 1961, 1964, and 1965, and of both leagues the latter two seasons. Through the decade no man had batted .300 or better every year from 1960 on, except Clemente. But Clemente had also established himself as far more than a great hitter. During a ball game in Los Angeles dead center in that fierce 1966 pennant struggle, the Dodgers got a runner on third base, with less than two out, and the next batter lofted a fly ball to right field. Clemente tensed under the ball, caught it as he moved forward, and then his strong lithe right arm whipped the ball home, to catcher Jim Pagliaroni. And the Los Angeles runner, on a team noted for its speed and crafty baserunning, anchored himself at third. He would not dare test Clemente's arm. In the broadcasting booth of the Dodgers, Vin Scully shouted, "If I owned a big league club, I'd order everybody off the field and put Roberto Clemente in the outfield all by himself in fielding practice, and let him throw the ball. How he can throw!"

Yes, how he can throw. Once he made a 420-foot throw to nip a runner at the plate. In that September run of 1966, in a single game against Milwaukee, he threw out two men on the bases in the first five innings. Three days earlier, he had fielded a base hit with the bases loaded, and suddenly the hit was not a hit. For Clemente fired the ball home, and a desperately sliding Jim Barbieri, of the Dodgers, was out at the plate.

How he can hit, how he can throw, how he can chase fly balls and catch them, how he can run. For this is one of the truly complete ballplayers of our time. He has, more than once, thrown out over 20 men on the base paths in a single season. He has raced from first to home on singles. He has caught fly balls no other right fielder could have reached. His ability to charge sinking line drives and snatch them off the grasstops is wondrous. His judgment of line drives rattled off Pittsburgh's tricky right-field wall is uncanny. And everything he does, he does with enormous style. Sportswriter Larry Merchant said it perfectly: "Fielding, throwing, running, or hitting, he swirls with the grace of a flamenco dancer, and castanets envelop him." With the exception of a young Willie Mays, no man in baseball plays with such flair, with such uncorked excitement.

The facets of Roberto Clemente are many, and they are bright. Baseball, today, appears to have become a game of painstaking science. Pitchers develop their craft like Renaissance artisans. New pitches are added to the already clustered repertoire. Sliders, hard and slow; change-ups, off the fast ball and off the curve; screwballs, fork balls, palm balls, sinkers, slip pitches, knuckle balls, and, of course, that new-old pitch, the "country sinker," which you and I know as the spitball.

In the field, managers continue to devise new defenses. When Lou Boudreau, as manager of the Cleveland Indians, moved his team's shortstop to the right side of second with Ted Williams at bat, a startled baseball world took note. Today such shifts are commonplace; Willie McCovey, Hank Aaron, and Willie Stargell see infields bunched against their strength each day. Alvin Dark, managing at Kansas City, chased his second baseman into the outfield when mammoth Frank Howard came to bat, and played with four outfielders.

But no matter how involved the game has become, it still remains basically a two-man game. The pitcher vs. the batter. And the average pitcher, though he may have more than a dozen different pitches—Juan Marichal employs thirteen—still finds he is forced to rear back and let fire his fast ball far more often than any other pitch in his bag of arrows. The average batter, though he may drag a bunt, though he may hit to the opposite field or chop down on the ball, hoping for a high bounder that he can beat out, still finds he must dig in and swing with all his force far more often than he ever tries to drop-shot a hit over the fingertips of a shortstop. Oh, there are exceptions. Matty Alou and Maury Wills try to finesse their way on, and Mike Cuellar and Phil Regan, among others, get men out on pitches that do not blaze by in a pale blur. Still, for all its intricacies and elegant strategies, baseball is a game of power.

Roberto Clemente digs in at the plate, his rear right foot as far back in the batter's box as the baseball law allows (and sometimes farther than that), and when a pitch is fired at his strike zone, he attacks it with all the fury of a tiger. His bat is a whiplash, his mouth twists in anger, his eyes are slitted at his target, and all he wants to do—at that moment—is crush a baseball. From the sound of it, that is what he apparently does do. Yes, he can throw and run and catch, but to the baseball fan and to the baseball pitcher, the enduring picture of Roberto Clemente is at the plate, attacking a baseball. Sometimes one hand leaves the bat and he clubs frantically at the ball, like a farmer axing a fleeing turkey. Sometimes both feet leave the ground and he leaps at the ball, like a prizefighter firing a savage left hook. But always it is a man on the attack.

How he can hit. He ripped 40 doubles in 1964, ten or more triples in 1955, 1958, 1961, 1965, 1966, and 1967, and over 200 hits in 1961, 1964, 1966, and 1967. For a spell in late 1966, he led all National Leaguers in runs batted in—Hank Aaron, Willie Mays, teammate Stargell, all these established sluggers trailed. When the year had ended, only Aaron, with 127, led Clemente's 119 rbi. The next year Clemente's 110 rbi trailed only Orlando Cepeda's 111. His base hits are bullets, either ground balls sizzled through a paralyzed infield, or line drives hung out like frozen rope, up the alleys in right-center or left-center field, or drilled on a rising line over the most distant fences. Baseball men have a tribute for hitters like Clemente: "They can fall out of bed on Christmas morning, and hit line drives."

For years it was said, Yes, Roberto Clemente is a fine hitter, a sharp hitter, a hitter for high average, but he has no power. Yet he drove a baseball into a howling wind at Candlestick Park in 1960 against Giant right-hander Sam Jones, the ball traveling 450 feet in the air, over the center-field fence. No ball had ever been hit as far in San Francisco, and Clemente hit his into the teeth of a gale. He smashed a home run over the left center-field wall at Wrigley Field that is one of the longest home runs ever hit in that park. Sandy Koufax will tell you that the longest ball he ever saw hit to the wrong field was a home run Clemente hit off Koufax, over the right center-field wall at the old Los Angeles Coliseum, where the fence was so removed from home plate it looked more like a one-iron golf shot than a baseball field.

Alvin McBean, a teammate and friend of Clemente's, says with pardonable exaggeration, "Clemente hit a ball 800 feet one afternoon in the Virgin Islands. There was no fence. The ball traveled 500 feet in the air, and then rolled downhill."

Yes, he has hit, and he has hit for power, but playing at Forbes Field, with the most distant fences in the league, Bob Clemente has tuned himself to his environment. The infield is baked hard, the grass clipped short as a chihuahua's fur; why not rip ground balls over that sleek surface? The outfielders must spread out to cover vast acreage; why not drill line drives between them?

And despite all the noise about home runs, games are

won by scoring runs, and you score more runs the old-fashioned way—with a series of base hits—than you do with one swish of the bat.

Yes, he can hit. Jim Davenport says, "Clemente has convinced me that he's the best hitter in this league." When Davenport said it, he was a teammate of Willie Mays.

Nor is this new. True, Clemente has shot to the fore of his league's hitters during the 1960s, but in his second season in the majors—1956—he hit .311. He was then barely old enough to vote. Injuries held him back those early years. He missed 143 games the first five years; he was sapped by colds, flu attacks, a nervous stomach that sent prickles of pain through his body, spasms of diarrhea, loose spinal discs, infected tonsils, bone chips in his throwing elbow, tension headaches. One of Clemente's legs is bigger than the other; his entire body is thrown out of kilter by this imbalance, and his spine has paid for the warping. Yet he got his 1,000th hit back in early August of 1961. He had to be doing something with the bat those first seasons. You don't get a thousand hits in the dugout or with your mouth. And when he made his 1,000th hit, to some teams and pitchers it appeared they had short-changed Clemente. Only a thousand? Seemed more like a million. Clemente's 1,000th hit came against Cincinnati, in a four-run first inning, and knocked young Ken Hunt out of the ball game. Umpire Mel Steiner called time, to present Clemente with the slightly used baseball, and out in the Reds' bullpen, relief pitcher Jim Brosnan remarked, "That's Roberto's one-thousandth hit," and Texan Bill Henry drawled laconically, "Did he get 'em all off us?"

No. It only seemed that way. Through the years, it has become a matter of inverted pride among rival ball clubs. Who's given up the most hits to Roberto Clemente? Why, *we* have. The Dodgers must be sure of it. In a five-year spell, Clemente batted .369 against Los Angeles, and two of those five years he was over .400. But Clemente plays no favorites. He hits 'em all.

Still, it is a many-faceted game, and he is a many-faceted ballplayer, and a many-faceted human being. He has his loves and his hates, his rages and his joys. He is dark-skinned, which in his native land of Puerto Rico is neither unusual nor stigmatizing. In mainland America, it marks Clemente, and he has paid for the mark. He is Puerto Rican, and though Puerto Ricans are American citizens, few mainland Americans realize this. Thus, he often has been made to feel like an outsider in this land. He has faced racial discrimination not only in the motels and restaurants of the South, where the Pirates train each year, but on his own ball club. And as a Latin American, he has faced the odd neglect from the fringe areas of baseball that equate skill on the diamond with geography and skin pigment. In 1966, Roberto Clemente spoke out against this condition:

"The Latin-American player doesn't get the recognition he deserves," Clemente was quoted in an Associated Press dispatch of August 23, 1966. "Neither does the Negro player, unless he does something really spectacular, like Willie Mays. We have self-satisfaction, yes. But after the season is over, nobody cares about us. Zoilo Versalles was the Most Valuable Player in the American League, but how many times has he been asked to make appearances at dinners or meetings during the winter? Juan Marichal is one of the greatest pitchers in the game, but does he get invited to banquets? . . . I am an American citizen, but some people act like they think I live in the jungle someplace."

Clemente was an embittered man at the moment, upset at what he considered a second-class status. "This is a matter of sports," he said, "of a man's ability and his accomplishments. What matters what language he speaks best?"

Each man has his own grudges. It is not really important to Roberto Clemente that he appear or not appear at baseball banquets. They are dull affairs at best, and they encroach on his time, his privacy. They make you fat and logy. Clemente is a family man. What he prefers doing, above all, is being with his lovely wife, Vera, and his two tiny sons, or with his parents, who live in a home bought for them by Clemente. But as Roberto Clemente climbs out of the rucks of neglect to which he had been assigned for many years, he must also become a spokesman for his people—for the Puerto Ricans and other Latin Americans in baseball, for the dark-skinned people everywhere in this nation, for the foreigners of this nation who speak a native tongue more fluently than they do English and are made to suffer for this talent. Yet how many mainland Americans speak Spanish half as well as Clemente speaks English? How many Americans have dared go to a distant land, and make good competing with the very finest men of that land? Orlando Cepeda, another Latin American who has made good playing ball in the States, spoke out once about the charge that Latin ballplayers are gutless. "We have enough guts just to come here," Cepeda said.

Roberto Clemente has also had the courage to come to the States, and face the people. Now he has climbed to the very top of his profession, competing in a foreign land. Before 1967, he signed a contract for $100,000 a year; few men have ever earned more in baseball. His success has enabled him to buy a splendid home in Río Piedras, and from his veranda the city of San Juan spreads out like a cluster of diamonds. He is in the athlete's prime of life.

Pressures—such as those produced by injury, either mental or physical—will not relent simply because he has prospered. If anything, they will intensify. And so the excitement Roberto Clemente brings to the baseball diamond is wrought by tensions of all sorts. He is the product of his times, and these are tense times, an age of psychological revelation, an age of racial revolution, an age of rising expectations for the downtrodden, an age of war.

But somehow, when Roberto Clemente climbs into the batter's box and sets himself deeply and solidly, his bat swinging back and forth like a pendulum or a massive golf club, his glittering eyes targeted on the pitchers, we forget that other world outside, the world of war and revolution. We strip away these excesses. What matters what language he speaks best? He speaks baseball. Baseball has its own tensions, its own dramas, and they have a purity that is elemental. Men rose out of caves not unlike baseball dugouts, men with clubs and men with rocks, and they faced each other just as batters face pitchers with their bats and baseballs. Evolution has made certain changes. The cavemen were clumsy louts. When Juan Marichal winds to throw his fast ball and Roberto Clemente tenses to meet it, we see savagery, yes, but we also see such skill as you are unlikely to find in nearly any other profession in the world.

So we will look at Roberto Clemente, in this book, as a man, yes, as a person, as a Latin American, as a man with a dark skin and with certain bitternesses and disappointments, but mainly we will look at Roberto Clemente, baseball's greatest hitter. It is enough.

2

"Hmm, Sounds Familiar"

THE ISLAND of Puerto Rico lies in the Caribbean Sea, warmed by the Gulf Stream and an unfrowning sun, yet cooled by ocean breezes. Frost and snow never visit the island, and a tropical garden of infinite variety and color flourishes lushly over the land. Royal poinciana trees blaze forth their bright red blossoms. Hibiscus blooms unfold until they are the size of dinner plates. Bougainvillea vines drape rooftops with their tiny crisp blood-red petals. The air is scented with jasmine. Mangoes, breadfruit, papayas, sapodillas fall in clusters about the feet, pulpy, sweet, juicy.

This is Roberto Clemente's home, an island slightly smaller than the state of Connecticut. Its name Puerto Rico means Rich Port. Sugarcane and pineapple grow swiftly and full from the dark earth.

Yet do not be lulled by the abundance of fruit and tree. This land is one of the most crowded places in the world. Many of its 2.6 million people live in incredibly tight quarters in the cities of the island, and though the slums are being torn down, the poor live poorly in Rich Port. And for all the soft ocean breezes and the scent of jasmine, each year tropical storms howl across the island and batter at thousands of flimsy homes; hurricanes make Puerto Rico a yearly stopover in July, August, September, October.

Yet the island continues to grow, and to grow strong. It has been part of the United States ever since the Spanish-American War of 1898, when America overthrew the Spanish Empire in the Caribbean, and Puerto Rico and Guam were ceded to the United States as war booty. Its ties with the United States are actually 400 years old, for it was Puerto Rico that Christopher Columbus set foot on, when he discovered America.

Today Puerto Rico is a commonwealth, a self-governing territory under the protection of the United States. Its citizens are citizens of the United States. When they sing their nation's anthem, they begin, "Oh, say can you see . . ." The island has been for years a showcase of democracy in the Caribbean. Its constitution is a model for emerging nations.

Still, the role of a nation under another nation's protectorship is not always happy. Orlando Cepeda once said to me, "When we were little, back home, the American Marines came down, the American soldiers and sailors. They were big and we were little, and they would get drunk on Saturday nights, and pick fights. We had to protect ourselves."

The presence of military contingents from the States was deemed necessary to protect American investment in Puerto Rico. For years, the largest sugar plantations on the island were owned by corporations in the United States. Native Puerto Ricans labored all day in the fields beneath a hot sun for $1 and $2 a day, to raise and support large families, and from the sweat of their labor, other Americans back on the mainland grew rich. Thus developed a sense of resentment, a feeling of oppression that has not been fully dissipated, though a process began in the 1940s of condemning great plantations, and much of the land was purchased from the Stateside corporate landholders.

The assimilation of Puerto Rico into the American nation is not complete, and many Puerto Ricans in this nation feel they are strangers, though the United States is their country just as much as it is the country of a Kansan or a Californian or a Connecticut Yankee. Not even military service under the Stars and Stripes has wiped out the feeling of difference. No fighting man acquitted himself more nobly or bled more profusely in defense of American freedom than Puerto Rico's brave 65th Infantry Regiment in the Korean War.

This sense of difference marks most Latin-American ballplayers. They speak freely of it. There are problems of race, of language, of adapting to the customs of a strange land. Habits are different, food is different, life—in all its aspects—is vastly different. Felipe Alou, from the Dominican Republic, has played baseball in the United States for over a decade, yet he says he thinks of himself as an "outsider," and Alou recalls bitterly how the governor of Louisiana would not permit him to play baseball on an otherwise all-white baseball team in a minor league early in Alou's career.

So when a Latin ballplayer's career in the United States is noted, let it also be noted that whatever he accomplished has come about in a strange and difficult land.

Roberto Clemente, of course, knew none of this when he was born on August 18, 1934, in the town of Carolina, a suburb of San Juan. Life was more pleasant for young

Roberto Walker Clemente than it was for many Puerto Rican children. His father was not a laborer in a sugar plantation, but the foreman of the plantation. Roberto's parents ran a grocery and a meat market for the plantation workers. Roberto's father also owned some trucks, which he used for small shipping jobs.

There were seven children, six boys and a girl. Roberto was the youngest. Latin-American families are very close, very protecting, very loving. The youngest is loved not only by his parents, but by his older brothers and sisters. Thus, Roberto was a well-cared-for child. Here, we would call it spoiled. There, it is "loved."

Though Roberto was born in the depression year of 1934, there was no depression in his family. "My father always worked," Clemente recalls. "We lived in a big wooden house, with a large front porch. Five bedrooms, living room, dining room, kitchen. Indoor bathroom."

Indoor bathroom. So many Latin-American families had no indoor plumbing, no water on their land at all. When he was a child in the Dominican Republic, Felipe Alou used to walk a mile to the river, and carry water on his head and shoulders, for the family.

Roberto had less difficult chores. In the summer, when his father would hire out his trucks for jobs, Roberto often helped out, loading or unloading sand. Not difficult, he insists.

But more important than the amount of physical labor were the attitude and atmosphere within the Clemente house.

"When I was a boy, I realized what lovely persons my mother and father were," Clemente has said. "I was treated real good. I learned the right way to live. I never heard any hate in my house. Not for anybody. I never heard my mother say a bad word to my father, or my father to my mother. During the war, when food all over Puerto Rico was limited, we never went hungry. They always found a way to feed us. We kids were first, and they were second."

As a boy, Roberto played ball every day. Mainly, it was softball, in playgrounds at first, and later in a municipal league. He played shortstop or he pitched. When he was not playing ball, he squeezed a hard rubber handball hour after hour, to strengthen the muscles in his throwing arm. Today, that arm is one of the strongest in baseball history.

When he did not play softball, he played sandlot baseball. And when he played neither, he often crouched over the family radio, listening to reports of ball games in the Puerto Rican winter league. His idol, when he was a youngster, was Monte Irvin, the slugging Giants' outfielder who played ball in Puerto Rico in the winter. Irvin did two things Clemente admired: Monte could hit, and Monte could throw. For a spell, Roberto's nickname was Monte Irvin.

If you think this obsession with baseball occasionally jangled his folks' nerves, you're right. Even in a permissive home where the children came first, Roberto's mother sometimes became edgy over her son's total occupation with ball.

"I would forget to eat because of baseball," Clemente says, "and one time my mother wanted to punish me. She started to burn my bat, but I got it out of the fire and saved it. Many times today she tells me how wrong she was and how right I was to want to play baseball."

But Clemente's mother did not always oppose her son's involvement. She couldn't. We read today of ballplayers who inherit their skills from their fathers. With Clemente, it was his mother who passed on the natural talent. Clemente says he got his arm from his mother. "She can still a ball from second base to home plate." Clemente ow his mother was invited to throw out the first ball e amateur winter league in Puerto Rico, back in 1963. "She was seventy-three at the time," Clemente says. "She threw the ball from a box seat to home plate. She had something on it, too."

Roberto intended to go to college and become an engineer. And though he says baseball was his life, at high school he managed to spread himself over other sports as well. He played baseball for his high school team, but he also made the track team, where he became an all-round sensation. Roberto threw the javelin; he high-jumped; he performed in what was then called the hop, skip, and jump, and which today is the triple jump. His best marks were outstanding. He tossed the javelin 195 feet; he high-jumped six feet; and he triple-jumped over 45 feet. Roberto Clemente was considered a sure member of Puerto Rico's Olympics squad for the 1956 event in Melbourne, Australia.

But professional baseball interfered with such a schedule. A high school history teacher, Roberto Marin, who also coached a softball team, became impressed with Clemente's skills. Marin passed the word to Pedro Zorilla, owner of the Santurce baseball team, in Puerto Rico, and one of the wisest judges of baseball talent in the Caribbean.

Zorilla shrugged off the unsolicited advice. Perhaps he had heard of too many high school phenoms from too many amateur scouts.

Later Zorilla took in a baseball game in the town of Manati, west of San Juan, where Zorilla lived. A seventeen-year-old center fielder caught his eye. Caught it? Filled it. The boy slammed a 390-foot triple and two doubles, and rifled a long throw to catch an opposing runner at third.

In the stands, Zorilla whistled. "Who is he?" he asked.

"His name is Roberto Clemente," a fan said.

"Hmm. Sounds familiar," Zorilla said.

Zorilla approached the boy he once could have had for nothing. This time he offered a bonus of $300. Elated, Roberto went home, but to his astonishment his parents said, "Not enough." Until then he had no idea they were aware of bonuses and other by-products of play.

Zorilla eventually agreed to pay Clemente a $500 bonus, plus $60 a month (and one free baseball glove), and Clemente put on a Santurce uniform while still in high school. The notion of attending college to become an engineer faded, once Clemente looked about at the other Santurce players. The team employed such men as Willie Mays, Orlando Cepeda, Ruben Gomez. Its manager was a former big league catcher, Herman Franks.

The idea that Latin Americans could not play big league ball also began to fade. Back in the States, Minnie Minoso had burst into stardom. In 1954, Bobby Avila would lead the American League in batting. More than any others, these two men—Minoso and Avila—brought sharply home to young Bob Clemente that a boy from the island might someday be a headlined performer on the mainland. "I thought Stateside players were better than Latin players," he has said. "I thought you had to be Superman to make it. But when Minoso and Avila made it big, I realized others could do it, too."

Clemente played at Santurce in the winters of 1952–53, 1953–54, and 1954–55. In his third season, he batted .356.

Even before that .356, big league scouts tailed Clemente. Al Campanis, of the then Brooklyn Dodger office, organized a clinic in Puerto Rico. Clemente was one of 100 prospects. As soon as Clemente began to hit and throw, to snare fly balls and run, Campanis—like Zorilla before him—had eyes for no one else. "Campanis asked me to do everything," says Clemente. "Run, hit, field, throw. Nobody else did anything."

Why should they have done anything? You wander into an old mine pit, and suddenly there is a single huge diamond in front of you, and you are rich indeed. No need to be a hog.

When the one-man show ended, Campanis suggested the boy join the Dodger farm system. Clemente's father turned down the idea. He wanted Roberto to finish high school.

More big league scouts clustered about the wiry youngster who rifled line drives to all fields, ran like the wind, and threw like—well, like nobody. During his senior year of high school in 1953, nine teams approached Clemente. They held fire until graduation. Then the Dodgers made a concrete offer: a $10,000 bonus for signing. It was one of the largest bonuses paid a Latin boy. It becomes particularly large when measured against the $200 paid Felipe Alou, the $500 given Juan Marichal.

Yet it might have been much bigger.

Clemente verbally and jubilantly accepted the Dodger offer of $10,000.

Later that same day, the Milwaukee Braves came along with a bonus of over $30,000.

The confused boy brought the dilemma home to his folks.

His mother said sternly, "If you gave the word, you keep the word."

Some things are more important than money. Honor, for one.

Clemente signed with the Dodgers.

Which is not to say he played with the Dodgers. He finished the winter league season at Santurce, and in the spring of 1954 joined a Dodger farm club.

Roberto Clemente was nineteen years old, just a youth. The Dodgers owned six minor league teams, and had working agreements with ten other clubs. Clemente could have been assigned to any of them. He might have begun at the very bottom, either at Class D Thomasville, of the Georgia-Florida League, or Shawnee, of the Sooner State League, or Union City, of the Kitty League, or Hornell, of the P.O.N.Y. League.

Clemente began, instead, at the top of the minor league pyramid. He joined former league pitching ace Joe Black, and future big leaguers Ken Lehman, Ed Roebuck, Chico Fernandez, Norm Larker, Sandy Amoros, and Gino Cimoli. This was the meat of the roster on the Montreal ball club, in the Triple-A International League.

Roberto Clemente was one short step from the big leagues.

3

"Take Care of Our Boy"

THE YOUNG MAN that joined the Montreal roster in 1954 stood five feet eleven inches and weighed a lean 175 pounds. Today Clemente is the same height, but he packs about ten more pounds into the spring of a baseball season, though he will wage a losing fight to keep most of those pounds through the dog days of August.

Other than that, he was very much like the Roberto Clemente we know today. Which is to say, he was physically suffering.

In 1953 Roberto Clemente tossed away the heavy bat he'd been using, and went to a lighter model. Styles in bats change nearly as much as styles in women's skirts. Bats have been thick-handled and thin-handled, bottle-shaped and straight, long and short, heavy and light. In the days of Babe Ruth, and before Ruth, home-run champion Gavvy Cravath, 50-ounce bats were not unique. Today they do not exist, nor do 40-ounce clubs, and the 32- and 33-ounce bat prevails. Sluggers today whip their light bats the way lion tamers slash away in a den of spitting cats.

Photographs of batters swinging at pitched balls reveal that the bat itself bends like a rubber-handled blackjack, or like a modern fiber-glass vaulting pole. The secret in hitting home runs today is getting the bat around on the ball, and whiplashing it. With a lighter bat, you come around more quickly, and with a thin handle you catapult the meaty end of the bat against the ball.

While at Santurce, Clemente noted that some of his teammates had switched to lighter weapons, and the ball suddenly had started to go out of sight. Ernie Banks would become a tremendous home-run hitter in the National League because he shifted to a lighter bat. Baseball hitters are a proud lot. They measure the distance of their blows the way anglers weigh their tarpon. Clemente, too, wanted to see baseballs disappear over the most remote fence.

He picked up a new light bat, he swung from his heels, and *pop*!

No, not the ball. His back. Out it flew, and the young man who entered the International League in the spring of 1954 was simply another human being with an aching back.

It was not his only mark. Back in the Puerto Rican League, outfielder Luis Olmo and Clemente's manager Herman Franks had coached the youngster in the art of basketmaking. Just as Willie Mays was learning in 1952 and 1953 to catch baseballs at his belt buckle instead of up around the eyes, so too was Clemente mastering the basket catch in the Puerto Rican League. It is not significant which came first, Mays' or Clemente's belly catches, the ball dropping neatly into the upturned basket of a big brown glove. (Neither came first. Bill Rigney caught pop flies at his belt when he was a Giant infielder a decade earlier, and a quarter of a century before that, Rabbit

Maranville practiced the basket catch in Boston.) What is significant is that the two greatest outfielders of our time catch fly balls that way. Genius has a way of striking out on independent and odd paths. Each man probably developed his style unaware of the other. Gentlemen, no patent squabbles.

Clemente's belt-buckle catches aren't. That is, Clemente lets the ball fall below his belt before he snatches it off, and there is a sliver of time you find yourself catching your breath as the ball continues to fall lower and lower. But fear not. The glove is there, and the ball is soon there, trapped somewhat left of center, and another putout has been recorded. Willie Mays has expounded on the advantages of such a method. It helps, Mays says, in getting rid of the ball quickly, on throws back to the bases. Clemente does not elaborate on his reasons. The chances are (for both men) there is no real reason, other than that it feels comfortable, and it adds an extra fillip to their already flamboyant styles.

Unfortunately, at Montreal, Roberto Clemente had few opportunities to put on display his basket catches. If baseball has become a more complicated game on the field, it is nothing compared to the hairsplitting legalistic gobbledygook behind the scenes, in what is called the front offices but in reality are shadowy backrooms, inaccessible and remote, except to tax attorneys and certified public accountants. In 1954 Roberto Clemente unwittingly became involved in this shadow play.

At the time, a first-year ballplayer who had received a bonus of at least $4,000 and had been sent to the minor leagues had to stay with his assigned minor league team for a full season. At the end of the first season, if the major league club wanted to make sure it still retained the young man, it had to promote him to its roster. If the major league club felt it was overburdened by such bonus ballplayers or just could find no room for this particular young man, it could keep him in the minors, provided no other big league club wanted him and was willing to pay a draft price of $4,000.

Confused? Naturally.

Not that the rule was purposeless. It had its reason. Big league baseball owners are not the most generous of men (to say the least), and a wealthy club would be delighted to find a young man in the cane thickets of Puerto Rico or Cuba or the Dominican Republic, pay him $4,000 or $5,000 (if it had to), assign him to a minor league team, and keep him three or four or five years, or longer, until he appeared ripe enough for the jump to the parent club. The wealthiest of clubs could buy unlimited numbers of young players for relative pittances, and keep them down on the farms until the established stars on the big league roster started to show their age. The poorer teams, naturally, could not compete with the more wealthy. A situation of the haves getting richer and the have-nots getting poorer would develop, and your first-division teams would soon be out of sight of your second.

Decades ago, Commissioner of Baseball Kenesaw Mountain Landis objected violently to this bit. He called it "covering up," and if he hated anything more than not seeing his name in the papers regularly, it was "covering up." To Landis it was no better than slavery, and to many people who have looked into the shenanigans of baseball, Landis was right.

Roberto Clemente fitted the above qualifications. He had been paid more than $4,000. He has been assigned to a minor league club. He would play there all that first season. The Dodgers, at the end of 1954, would face the problem of bringing him up—to a roster already choked with great players—or else making him vulnerable to draft by another club.

Naturally big league owners do not like seeing a man whom they have paid—in Clemente's case—$10,000, and whom they have spent a year in seasoning, snatched off for a measly $4,000 by a rival club. If ballplayers have pride, club owners have vanity. Nothing so tweaks that vanity as seeing a lost prospect beating your brains out through the next decade.

Not that the Dodgers yielded up Clemente easily.

Clemente played his first full season at the Dodger farm in Montreal. That is, he was on the roster all the season. But in reality he played little more than a fourth of the season. True, he got into 87 games, but in many of those games he was restricted to a pinch-hitting appearance, if he was not running for a tired pitcher, or trotting to right field for defensive purposes in a late inning. In 87 games, the average starting ballplayer will bat over 300 times. Clemente batted 148 times.

It is Clemente's contention that the Dodgers put him on ice, to protect him from the draft. No big league club likes to buy a pig in the poke. Clemente insists that Dodger owner Walter O'Malley told Montreal Royal manager Max Macon to hide Roberto so he would remain an unknown quality to outsiders.

"If I struck out," Clemente recently told writer Myron Cope, of the days at Montreal, "I stay in the lineup. If I played well, I'm benched. One day I hit three triples and the next day I was benched. Another time they took me out for a pinch hitter with the bases loaded in the first inning."

Under such circumstances, the youngster did not show much on the field. In his 148 times at bat, he batted .257. Nor was there much power. Of his 38 hits, five were doubles, three triples, and two home runs. He drove in twelve runs. He stole one base. On occasion, Max Macon inserted the young man at third base. It was not exactly a shining showcase.

Clemente bore other problems. "I had studied English in high school," he has said,"but I was not able to speak until I began to talk to players [in Montreal]. Not speaking the language is a terrible problem."

He faced another problem, totally new to him. Back on the island, Clemente had seen only a carefree mingling of the races. Now he learned of racial separation, unyielding lines drawn between dark- and light-skinned people. One of the teams in the International League was Richmond, Virginia, capital of the old Confederacy. "At Montreal," Clemente recalls, "when we went on the road, I could not stay with the white players in Richmond. I felt it was childish."

He saw how cliques were formed along racial lines. He says, "The first thing the average white Latin-American player does when he comes to the States is associate with other whites. He doesn't want to be seen with Latin Negroes, even ones from his own country, because he's afraid people might think he's colored." Clemente did not have this possible out. His skin was dark.

All this went into the making of that first season. The Dodgers undoubtedly were aware of pressures on the young man. Still, baseball is a cold-blooded profession. What the Dodger scouts also saw was a young man who had more than a tendency to swing at bad balls. It was an obsession. Clemente also seemed troubled by curve balls, and there is a report Roberto even manifested difficulty in going back for balls hit over his head, although it is hard to imagine this defensive genius misplaying fly balls. And Clemente stubbornly, and perhaps correctly, insists none of the flaws counted. The Dodgers just wanted to keep him under wraps, away from prying eyes of rival scouts.

The draft rule operates to counteract the haves remaining haves, and the have-nots remaining in last place. At the draft meeting, the club with the worst won-lost record in the preceding season has first choice of all the bonus players still on minor league rosters.

In the early 1950s, the Pittsburgh Pirates were the worst team in baseball. Some say they were the worst ever to play baseball. During the 1954 season, Pirate scouts diligently went up and down the farms, searching for bonus boys who might be available the coming winter, unprotected by their owners.

On one such trip in the spring of 1954, Pirate president Branch Rickey, most astute judge of raw baseball talent in the history of the game, sent Pirate pitching coach Clyde Sukeforth to Richmond, Virginia, when Montreal came to town. Ostensibly, Sukeforth went to look at Montreal pitcher Joe Black, a relief ace of a few years prior, but who, like so many relief pitchers, had suddenly found he could no longer get the big leaguers out. Black was with Montreal, and Sukey sallied forth to see whether Black had perhaps picked up a new pitch or two that might help him regain his mastery.

Sukeforth is a man himself who might have been said to be seeking his old mastery. Back in 1951, when Clyde was the pitching coach for the Brooklyn Dodgers, his manager Charley Dressen one afternoon phoned the bullpen and asked Sukeforth which of two pitchers toiling out there seemed most ready. Sukeforth promptly said, "Branca," and two pitches later Ralph Branca threw a fast ball on the fists, and Bobby Thomson hit it into the left-field seats of the Polo Grounds, for a pennant-winning home run in one of the most exciting moments in all of baseball.

Withal, Clyde Sukeforth has not only been a most wise judge of pitching, but a well-rounded baseball man.

So Sukeforth's visit to Richmond may have sent a premonitory thrill through Dodger channels. Word may have filtered out to keep Roberto Clemente well hidden. When Sukeforth showed up, he immediately trained his eyes on Joe Black, and it did not take long to convince the coach that for whatever reason—the Pirates did not want Black. Still, Sukeforth was in Richmond, the Virginia hospitality was pleasant, and why not watch a few games? Though it was true that if he wanted to see Bob Clemente play baseball, he would have had to look hard and fast those few days, Sukeforth nonetheless managed to see quite a bit of Clemente, and at the coach's leisure. Sukeforth came to the ball park early to watch batting practice and fielding practice, and in no time at all—just as Al Campanis needed no time—Sukeforth was hypnotized by the lithe grace of the outfielder, by the line drives ripped off his bat, by the power and accuracy of his throwing arm.

When Sukeforth left Richmond, he said to Max Macon, "Take care of our boy," and both men knew Sukey wasn't talking about Joe Black.

If you wonder why Sukeforth so brazenly alluded to Clemente as an object of Pittsburgh desires, the answer lies in the roster of the Brooklyn Dodgers. In 1955 the Dodgers would field one of the most powerful teams in National League history. Its pitchers included Carl Erskine, Billy Loes, Russ Meyers, Don Newcombe, Johnny Podres, Clem Labine, Erv Palica, Ed Roebuck, and a young kid named Sandy Koufax. Roy Campanella handled the catching. The infielders were Gil Hodges, Jim Gilliam, Pee Wee Reese, and Jackie Robinson, with such as Don Hoak, Charley Neal, Chico Fernandez, and Don Zimmer in reserve. The outfielders were led by Duke

Snider and Carl Furillo, with a third spot to be filled by Sandy Amoros. Gino Cimoli, Walt (Moose) Moryn, and George Shuba battled for a place on the squad.

On that Dodger roster there would be no room for Roberto Clemente, and Clyde Sukeforth knew it.

Another reason for not calling up Clemente has been hinted at over the years. The Dodgers, first big league team to hire a Negro ballplayer, would have eight Negroes on the 1955 roster. Ball clubs are sensitive to the racial make-up of their rosters. To them it is not a question of discrimination, but a question of economics. Baseball executives have said, off the record, they worry about what they call the "saturation" problem, the problem—as they see it—of too many Negroes on their team. The fear, they say, is that white spectators will stop coming to see ball teams where Negroes outnumber whites. In 1965, *Sport* magazine touched on this problem in an article dealing with professional basketball. If the problem is considered worthy of national editorial discussion long after such artists as Bill Russell, Wilt Chamberlain, Elgin Baylor, and Oscar Robertson have come along to make basketball a magnificent and thrilling spectator sport, you can imagine how jittery some sports executives may have been a decade earlier.

In any event—and it is likely the Dodgers mainly concerned themselves with such prosaic problems as a yen for swinging at bad balls—Roberto was not called up when the 1954 season had ended.

On Monday, November 22, 1954, baseball held its draft meeting in New York City. Other events caught the national eye that day—Dr. Samuel H. Sheppard was on trial in Cleveland, Ohio, for the murder of his wife; Premier Pierre Mendes-France thought he was moving ever closer to a Western European union with England; and Senator

Joe McCarthy rested comfortably in a hospital, after a sliver of glass had been removed from his elbow.

Pittsburgh, as expected, made the first selection, and the next day's papers referred to their choice as a "highly touted sleeper." His name was Roberto Walker Clemente.

Kansas City drafted three men from the minor leagues, including a pitcher named Cloyd Boyer, whose kid brother Ken would be joining the Cardinals that year, brought up from the St. Louis farm in Houston. There were other drafts, most of whom have since drifted into obscurity. The Cubs bought outfielder Jim King; the Giants drafted catcher Mickey Grasso.

Still, the number one choice had been Roberto Clemente. And what was Clemente's reaction to all this attention?

"I did not even know where Pittsburgh was," he has since said.

4

"Nice Guys Finish Last—And Not-Such-Nice Guys"

WHERE WAS PITTSBURGH? Last place; that's where. It had finished last in 1952, 1953, and 1954. In 1954 while Roberto Clemente was toiling at Montreal, the Pirates were compiling a record of 53 wins and 101 losses, a full eleven games behind the next-to-last Chicago Cubs.

Its manager those days was Fred Haney, a man of even temperament and exceptional baseball knowledge. But when a team finishes last three times running, or limping, and soon makes it four, something has got to go, and in baseball, it usually is the manager. Infielders mess up ground balls, pitchers throw hanging curves, runners stumble along the base paths like geriatric cases, batters pop up with the bases loaded, and the manager gets fired.

Not quite yet. Which is worse. When a manager is on his way out, nothing is so uncertain as his last days. You know he has to go, but there he is, still posting the lineup, still meeting the press after each loss, painfully answering questions. He is marking time, and so is the team, 25 men wandering about a ball field in a state neither of waking nor of sleeping, but a little of each.

This was the Pirate team Clemente joined in the spring of 1955. A close look at the 1954 club tells the story. Pittsburgh was last in hitting and last in pitching. Last by miles. The club batting average was .248; next was Cincinnati, at .262. No other team in the league had fewer than 2,000 total bases. The Pirates had 1,783. The Pirates scored over 100 runs less than anybody else. The team was last in times at bat, hits, two-base hits, and home runs. It stole 21 bases all season, lowest in the majors. And though they never seemed to get anybody on, they managed to leave 1,145 base runners, third worst in the league. Today we think of the Pirates as lacking in pitching depth, lacking in home-run power, but making up for it in slickness, particularly around second base. In 1954, its double-play combination was Curt Roberts at second and Gair Allie—no relation to Gene Alley—at short. Roberts batted a towering .232, but what he lacked in average he couldn't make up in power. Roberts hit one home run in 134 games. His partner, Allie, hit .199.

The pitching was no better. The Pirates scored 557 runs in 1954; its staff gave up 845. Its combined earned-run average was 4.92. It hurled a grand total of four shutouts. Just as its hitters were at the bottom of the heap, of the three starting pitchers in the league with earned-run averages over 5.00 runs per game, two were Pirates. Vernon Law's 5.50 was the worst among regular pitchers, though the Pirates also had guys like Len Yochim, with 7.20, and Laurie Pepper, with 7.94, among those who did not pitch 154 innings.

Yet great feats occurred when Pittsburgh played. When the Dodgers committed a triple steal on April 23, it was against Pittsburgh. When Harvey Haddix became the league's first ten-game winner, on June 13, he did so blanking the Pirates, 5–0. When Cincinnati made a triple play, on August 27, it was on a ground ball hit by Pirate catcher Jack Shepard. In the 1954 All Star game, the only Pirate who saw action was outfielder Frank Thomas. Thomas struck out.

Pittsburgh plopped into last place on April 29, and never twitched thereafter.

Losing breeds its own infections. The Pirates had come to be thought of as perpetual losers, a team that would lose twice as often as it won. You could bet on it. Soon the players themselves began to believe they could not win. The manager knew he could not win. And the fans, knowing their club would not win, stopped coming to the field. This was the worst, not just because an empty ball park lends a ghoulish atmosphere to the goings-on below, like the rattling of small bones in a large casket. The reason is more basic, more dollars-and-cents. To build anew takes money. You must buy up those young men on the farms. You must bid for the strong-armed college youths who throw baseballs through brick walls or hit them over the light towers. You must spend the hundred thousand dollars necessary to buy last season's 20-game winner or .300 hitter or fielding whiz. But if nobody comes to the games, there is no money, and you shuffle through the days of each summer hopelessly mired, a team marking time, a team going nowhere, a club going broke.

In 1954 home attendance for the Pirates totaled 475,494, worst in the league. Cincinnati, in seventh place, was next, with 704,167. You could squeeze by with 700,000; you can't with 475,000. The Pirate break-even point in the early and mid 1950s was close to 700,000 fans. With 475,000, the club lost half a million dollars.

It has been said, facetiously, that the team's talent lay in its vice-presidency, a man named Harry Lillis Crosby, better known as Bing. But it is facetious. The club was run by Branch Rickey, and the game has never known a more brilliant executive. Its manager, Fred Haney, later proved himself a superb field leader at Milwaukee, and still later, an inventive and shrewd general manager with the Los Angeles Angels.

But talent upstairs is not talent on the field, and by the end of 1954 the Pirates were in a sad fix.

Roberto Clemente was in an equally sad fix. One of his brothers had developed an incurable brain tumor. When the 1954 season ended, Robert visited his dying brother in a San Juan hospital. He left the hospital and got into his car, and at an intersection a few blocks away, another car, a drunk at the wheel, smashed into Clemente's car at 60 miles an hour. The impact jarred loose three spinal discs in Clemente's back.

And so it was a grieving young man, with a perpetually painful back, that reported to his first Pirate training camp at Fort Myers, Florida, prior to the 1955 season.

At Fort Myers, other problems assailed the twenty-year-old rookie. The accommodations at Fort Myers—a small town on the Gulf Coast of Florida just above the cypress swamps—were segregated, and remained so until the 1960s. When Clemente ventured from the camp, he found he had to eat in restaurants for Negroes only. When the club went on the road to play other teams training in Florida, he stayed in motels for Negroes only.

"It is silly," Clemente says today about such practices. "It is childish. I feel strongly about it. Through 1964, you couldn't eat anyplace, except at Howard Johnson's. Segregation will have to go."

It is going, but in 1955 it remained a sturdy southern

convention. In the North, things were not much better. And on the Pirates, things definitely were not better.

"There was trouble with the players," Clemente recalls. "They would make smart remarks about Negroes, to me. I would make them back to them. Not behind my back. Right to my face."

Nice guys, they say, finish last. Perhaps after they finish last a few years in a row, they cease being nice guys.

Whatever the problems, Clemente understood why he was in Fort Myers. To play ball. And so did the Pirates realize their role. The year 1955 did not do much to change the image of the Pirates, but subtle currents were at work. For one thing, there was all that youth. And if Roberto Clemente felt alienated by some of his teammates, he must have felt at home with others. Outfielder Felipe Montemayor came up from Mexico. Outfielder Roman Mejias was a Cuban. Dick Hall, a Pirate pitcher and part-time outfielder, spoke Spanish. The trail blazed by such as Minnie Minoso and Bobby Avila had its legion of followers. The Latin had become an integral part of American baseball.

Pittsburgh spent most of its exhibition season playing the Baltimore Orioles, in their second year after taking over the old St. Louis Browns' franchise. The Orioles had finished seventh in 1954, which did not make them the New York Yankees, but did provide some means of comparison. In 1955 the Pirates whipped the Orioles nine times in 14 meetings. More, the Pirates ended in second place in the Grapefruit League, percentage points behind the Milwaukee Braves. Milwaukee posted a 14-and-9 record, Pittsburgh a 17-and-12.

So a faint spark of confidence could be sensed in Pittsburgh when the 1955 season opened.

The spark was quickly snuffed. The Pirates were scheduled to open on April 12, in Brooklyn. Rain washed out the game. The next day was drippy, but they played. The Dodgers whipped Pittsburgh, 5–1, Carl Erskine besting Max Surkont.

In that delayed opener, the Pirate outfield was Frank Thomas in left, Tom Saffell in center, and Roman Mejias in right. Clemente rode the bench.

Clemente did not play the second game, either, nor the third, and Pittsburgh dropped three straight. Earl Smith, up from Phoenix, played in center one day, and the next day Smith and Felipe Montemayor shared center field, with Mejias and Thomas on the flanks.

The Pirates played their home opener, and Roberto Clemente was unveiled in a Sunday doubleheader, April 17, against the Dodgers, before a good crowd of 20,499.

It wasn't much of a debut for the Pirates. They lost both contests, 10–3 and 3–2.

But Clemente made quite a splash. He came to bat for the first time in the opening inning, two men out, nobody on, and young left-hander Johnny Podres on the mound. The Dodgers of 1955 broke all records by winning their first ten games. In no time they had made a shambles of the pennant race. This was the ball club that once owned Roberto Clemente.

Podres pitched, and Clemente ripped a single off the glove of shortstop Pee Wee Reese. A moment later, Frank Thomas tripled to right center, and Clemente had made the first hit and first run in Pittsburgh. Clemente went hitless his remaining three at bats in the first game, playing right field. In the second contest Roberto led off, and played center. Fred Haney would move the youngster back and forth all season, lead-off spot, third spot, sometimes as far down as sixth. Clemente had a single and a double in four trips. He scored a run, and at the end of his first playing day he was hitting .375.

The next day the Pirates were in New York, and kept right on losing. The Giants massacred the Pirates, 12–3, before 2,915 disinterested fans. But Clemente had a second fine day. Don Liddle, the little left-hander, was the Giant pitcher. Clemente hit an inside-the-park home run, added a sacrifice fly for two runs batted in, and in the field flashed the first sign of his great throwing ability. He snatched off a line drive in right field, and when a Giant runner was slow in returning to first, fired a perfect throw to Preston Ward, for a double play.

He had a hit the next day, but it was washed out—and a Pirate lead of 3–0 with it—when rain canceled the game with the Giants after three innings. He had a triple the next day, and for eight innings it looked as though the Pirates would win one, but in the ninth the Phils scored five runs, and won, 5–4. Clemente sat out the next game, as old Murry Dickson spun a four-hitter, beating Pittsburgh 8–0, which matched the Pirate record of eight losses and no wins.

The losing streak finally ended. On a Sunday doubleheader in Philadelphia, Clemente had a single and a double in the first game, knocking in two runs, and the Pirates won, 6–2. Then they reverted. The Phils blanked Pittsburgh, 2–0. But Clemente had another hit, and now he was hitting .360, seventh best in the young league.

That was the week that was, from Sunday to Sunday, Clemente's first week in the majors. You cannot tell what a man will do, from a week's effort. The pitchers did not know the young man. Nor was he easy to know. He had a trait fairly common to hitters up from Latin America. He loved to swing. If the ball was in his strike zone, he swung, and his strike zone included everything from eyeballs to shoetops, from the first-base dugout to the third.

But Clemente was hitting what he was swinging at, so it seemed no good to throw bad balls, hoping he'd fish. He would fish, and he'd land.

Other pitchers noticed something else. Clemente's head bobbed when he swung, so violently did he rip into a pitch. With the bobbing head, he took his eye off the ball. Pitchers began to change speeds, hoping to catch Clemente off balance, head moving, eyes not trained on the target.

On the Pirate bench, coach George Sisler noticed the same trait. Patiently he began to work with Clemente. Sisler was one of the great batting stylists of all time. In 15 years he compiled a batting average of .340. It might have been higher. Failing eyesight troubled Sisler his final seasons. In 1920, with the St. Louis Browns, Sisler batted .407, with a still-unmatched 257 hits. Two years later he topped it with a .422 average. Sisler was the classic batter, a man who waited with quiet bat, swung with short smooth stroke, and insisted that the ball be over the plate before he'd waste strength on it. His place in the Hall of Fame is secure, for Sisler not only was a great hitter, some think him the finest fielding first baseman of all time.

All through 1955, Sisler worked on Clemente's bobbing head and on Clemente's joyous style of swinging at anything in sight. Sisler batted .500 in the coaching league. Clemente's head no longer bobs (though his feet move about impatiently, sometimes one, sometimes the other, sometimes both leaving the ground during a swing), but Clemente still likes to swing. Actually he has cut down somewhat. In the first years it was almost impossible to walk Clemente. Today he will walk 40 times a season.

The great start, of course, did not last. It never does.

Men who find themselves batting .440 on April 30 often struggle to hit .240 by September 30. Still, you did not have to be a baseball seer to tab Clemente a hitter, if not now, then in the future. He had two hits off the Cubs' left-hander, Paul Minner, and raised his average to .367, before Gerry Staley, and Cincinnati, finally blanked him and ended a seven-game hitting streak. And on the third successive Sunday doubleheader, Clemente had a field day. This time he banged out a triple and four singles in nine trips, and two days later, batting lead-off against the great Warren Spahn in Pittsburgh, Clemente hit Spahnie's second pitch of the game over the left-field scoreboard, as Pittsburgh began a modest winning streak.

When he didn't hit—as he didn't, the next night—he still made himself known. The Pirates went into the ninth inning against Milwaukee, leading 5–3, but the Braves scored a run, and put men on second and third, with two out and big bespectacled George Crowe at bat. Crowe ripped a pitch on a line, headed for the right-field seats, but Clemente leaped and one-handed the ball to save the game. The next day, the team made a triple play and beat Milwaukee again, 4–0, and Clemente was 2-for-2, a single and a double, plus a sacrifice fly and a stolen base. The Giants came to town, and Clemente blasted a 430-foot triple off Johnny Antonelli to help win, 3–2. Newsmen began to wonder, were the Pirates for real? And if so, why? One answer, a writer suggested, lay in their youth. The starting lineup of that 3–2 win over the Giants averaged 23.9 years per man.

They weren't for real. Right after the win streak, the club lost 11 in a row, and that sealed its finish. It was to be last again, and Roberto Clemente who was hitting .360 after a week in the big leagues would end up 105 points below that, at .255.

Still, the season had its glorious moments for the young man whose aching back periodically put him on the bench for a couple or three days at a stretch. He caught a fly ball and threw out a Milwaukee runner trying to score on May 11, for his second double play of the year, and in a stretch of five days had four throwing assists. On May 24, 1955, he faced a man with whom his career was curiously laced—Joe Black—and Clemente ripped a two-run single through Black's legs into center field, in a 15–1 rout of the Dodgers.

He had three singles in a 12–3 win over St. Louis on June 2, and three singles the next day against Cincinnati. He blasted triples in two successive innings off Ed Roebuck, to help beat Brooklyn, 7–5, on June 30.

He sprained his right ankle in practice on May 26 and sat out four games, and in one of them the Pirates reverted to the Pirates of old. Even to the Giants of old. In the last half of the ninth inning of a 4–4 game, the Pirates had Tom Saffell on third base and young Gene Freese on first, with Roman Mejias at bat. Mejias walloped a clean base hit to center field, and Tom Saffell crossed the plate with what appeared to be the winning run. Hundreds of Pirate fans drifted onto the field, and even the umpires headed for the dressing room. But in center field, the Phils' Richie Ashburn noticed that Gene Freese had swerved off the base paths once he had seen Saffell score. Ashburn hurried the ball to Roy Smalley, and the Phil infielder stepped on second base, to force Freese. The game continued after the field had been cleared. Shades of Fred Merkle! And shades of John McGraw! In an earlier inning, when Phillie pitcher Bob Miller came to bat with a man on first, Pirate manager Fred Haney decided to make it difficult for the young man to sacrifice. He brought an outfielder into his infield, and faced Miller with five infielders. Miller promptly lined a base hit to the vacated outfield spot. After all this, in the eleventh inning the Phils scored four runs and won, 8–4. Why not?

Clemente returned to action the next day. You cannot get well on the bench this way. So he got well at bat. He had his first five-hit game, but not his last.

Clemente ripped two singles and three doubles in five times up; he scored two runs and drove in another, and led the Pirates to an 8–3 lead when curfew suspended the game in the bottom of the seventh. So even this was typical of the Pirates. They did not win the one-sided ball game until six weeks later, when the two teams played out the remaining innings.

But all was not fine, and everyday not a five-hit day, not when you bat .255. Clemente had his pained moments, too. He made occasional errors; he ran through stop signs; he went hitless not for a day, but for days at a time. Early in June, Spahn and Bob Buhl horse-collared him in nine at bats in a doubleheader. The next day he was 0-for-3; then he went 1-for-4, 0-for-4, and again 0-for-4, and in the stretch had a single in 24 times at bat. He was in the lineup the day Sad Sam Jones hurled his no-hitter against Pittsburgh, in Wrigley Field. As a matter of fact, Clemente was smack in the middle of the only excitement of the afternoon. Jones, with a toothpick between his teeth, fired his fast balls and jagged curves past the Pirates all day, until the ninth inning when his control fled, and Pirates Gene Freese, Preston Ward, and Tom Saffell all walked, with no out.

The next three hitters were Dick Groat, Roberto Clemente, and Frank Thomas.

Groat fanned.

Clemente took two quick strikes, then fouled two pitches, and swung and missed at a sweeping curve ball.

Thomas fanned.

Which epitomized the season. Yes, they had their moments, and they made their run for a brief spell, winning five and six games in a row, threatening to end out of the cellar at long last. They had youth and a show of speed, a flash of life, and they had in Roberto Clemente a hint of what might yet be. But when it was over, there they were, dead last.

No, that isn't fair, Last, yes. But not dead. Nobody knew it—yet—but through the next decade, the Pirates would never again finish last.

For Clemente it was a good beginning. Not great, but good. Roberto batted his .255, appearing in 124 games. Of his 121 hits, 23 were doubles, 11 were triples (testimony to his speed and power, both) and five were home runs. He knocked in 47 runs; he stole two bases.

Fans did not yet scream "*Arriba!*" when he came to bat. Kids did not mob him on the street or in restaurants, as they later would. He was just a talented youngster, earning his minimum salary of $6,000. He lived in Pittsburgh with a Mr. and Mrs. Stanley Garland. Garland was a post office employee; his wife was a nurse. Later, Clemente would say of the Garlands, "They have been like another father and mother to me."

And if the kids did not mob him in the streets, they at least would ask him for his autograph, as they asked all players. Clemente would oblige, signing patiently until all had been satisfied. There are some who think Clemente's popularity today with Pittsburgh fans stems from this simple act—signing autographs without saying, "No. I have to run. I have a bus to make." Or whatever players say when they are bored with kids shoving pieces of paper in their faces.

Clemente says of all this, "I was lonely. Why not sign? People remember you if you are nice to them."

5

"Get Out of My Way"

EVEN LOSING TEAMS have their dynasties. In the days of the early 1950s, you couldn't think of the Pittsburgh Pirates without thinking of Branch Rickey. Rickey, who had made the St. Louis Cardinals of the 1930s, the man who had more than any other developed the farm system, the man who had signed the first Negro to play major league ball. But dynasties must end; time is the great mover and remover in baseball as in other aspects of life.

After the 1955 season, seventy-four-year-old Branch Rickey stepped out of active direction of Pirate affairs. He became chairman of the board, more an honor than a duty. His place as general manager was taken by a man exactly half his age, Joe L. Brown. Young Brown had enough distinction going for him. He was the son of Joe E. Brown, the famous movie comedian, and a man always interested in baseball. It was Joe E. who had played the title role in the film version of Ring Lardner's famous base-ball short story, *Alibi Ike*, one of the few baseball films that did not embarrass true ball fans. Brown obviously knew his way about a ball field.

So did and does his son. Joe L. Brown has directed the Pirates ever since.

One of young Brown's first moves was to change managers. Not that Brown blamed Fred Haney for the cellar finishes of his Pirate teams. But something must be done to break the dispiriting cycle. Even if the flesh of the players does not change, the spirit can. Brown reached into the Pacific Coast League, where the Pirates owned the Hollywood Stars, and selected Hollywood manager Bobby Bragan to be that spirit changer. It was a splendid choice, if spirit changing is what baseball is all about. Perhaps it would be better if it was. Baseball would then be a game again. For all of the wonderful zest inherent to baseball, for all its life and color, there are men who must regard it not as a sport, but as a business. Businesses are not run by spirit; they are run by cold reason. The men who run businesses have little love for fun and games; they have, instead, an abiding respect for economics. Perhaps the two can be melded—a wise and fiscally aware mind, and a joyous or at least a lively spirit. It happens seldom; usually you have one or the other. In Bobby Bragan, Brown found zest. Oh, boy, he found it.

On the second day of the 1956 season, Bobby Bragan let it be known he ran the team. Bragan is not a man who loses equably. The Pirates had lost the opener, 4–3. Baseball men hate to lose by one run. Now the Pirates were engaged in a second tight contest. In a middle inning, the Pirates' opponents had a man on second. A base hit followed, and the man on second rounded third and headed home. A Pirate outfielder fired the ball home. But first baseman Dale Long cut off the throw, and permitted the run to score unchallenged. In the dugout, Bragan flushed with anger. Later, in the eighth inning, with Pirate Johnny O'Brien on third, and Pittsburgh trailing by one run, Bragan, who coached at third base, flashed a squeeze bunt sign to the batter. The batter did not see the bunt sign and instead swung away, and the Pirates failed to score. The batter was Roberto Clemente.

After the game—a 5–4 loss—Bragan announced he had fined both Long and Clemente $25 each, Long for needlessly cutting off the throw and giving up a run, and Clemente for missing the bunt signal.

Long's reaction differed from Clemente's. Long said he was glad Bragan had fined him. It would make a better player of him.

Clemente said not a word.

The Pirates played another one-run game the next day. Except this time they beat the Giants, 3–2.

The Pirates of 1956 were an odd crew. Streaky. All season long they would lift the hearts of Pirate fans by running off with four and five wins in a row. Now they're moving, fans would think. And just as swiftly they'd drop five, six, even eight straight, and the move was to the rear.

But the show of life was more real than that. And two big moves by the Pirate front office in 1956 changed the club. Besides all the pitching problems that most teams have—starters who don't finish, pitchers who develop sore arms or mysterious viruses, and relief pitchers who come in with the bases loaded and promptly fire a wild pitch—the Pirates had three glaring weaknesses. One was behind the plate, one at second base, and the other in center field. It is a baseball aphorism that a team is only as strong as its down-the-middle defense: catcher, pitcher, short-second combination, and center field. The Pirates were deficient both at the plate and behind it. They had no second baseman, and had found wanting a series of center fielders.

On May 16, 1956, the Pirates obtained young Bill Virdon, St. Louis Cardinal center fielder. For nearly a decade, Virdon was to be one of the finest of defensive outfielders, and a sharp and consistent hitter. Later that year, the Pirates reached into their Hollywood farm and came up with a second baseman. And what a second baseman! This was nineteen-year-old tobacco-chewing Bill Mazeroski, an almost silent ballplayer, with velvet moves, quick agile wrists, and in recent years, a most dangerous bat. Two of the three glaring weaknesses had suddenly grown into strengths.

Coincident with Virdon's purchase, the club began to win. Soon its record was 15 wins and 12 losses, and in a tightly bunched league, Pittsburgh was one game out of first place. It played a Sunday doubleheader at home on May 20 before 32,346 fans, largest crowd in five years, and the Pirates responded to the rare sight of a capacity house by belting the Braves 6–3 and 5–0. Bob Friend was a winning pitcher. The year before he had won 14 games, and his earned-run average of 2.84 was the best in the league, the first time in the league's history a pitcher for a last-place team had led in e.r.a.

But the real reason for the surge was Dale Long. Long had cheerfully accepted Bragan's tongue-lashing and $25 fine. It would make him a better player, he'd said. Darned if it—or something—didn't. Long went off on a home-run binge unexcelled in all of baseball's records. For eight straight days he hit home runs. His batting average soared to .414, his slugging percentage went out of sight, in excess of .800. Slugging percentages are figured by dividing times at bat into total bases, and total bases are, of course, computed on the basis of four for a home run, three for a triple, and so on. Men lead the league in slugging percentages these years with marks of .600 or so.

Long's eighth home-run day, on May 28, whipped the Dodgers 3–2, and the Pirates were a half game out of first. Long's contract was torn up and a new one written, with a hefty pay boost.

The Pirates kept winning. Long could not keep hitting home runs, nor could he maintain a .414 average, but he hit well, and so did other Pirates, among them Bob Clemente. Bob Friend moved his mark to seven wins and two losses, and when the All Star game would come along, Bob Friend would be the National League starting —and winning—pitcher, blanking the American League over the first three innings.

In June, Pittsburgh took over first place. Nobody believed this was where they would end, not even the ebullient Mr. Bragan. In a candid interview early in June, Bragan said he was aiming for fifth place. Why not? That would be up three notches over 1955, and it would mean the Pirates definitely were on the upgrade. Meanwhile, first place was heady, even if short-lived.

On June 9, Bob Clemente had become the fourth leading hitter in the league, with a .348 average. Four days later he'd boosted the mark to .357 and now he was third, behind the Cardinals' Rip Repulski at .378, and Clemente's teammate, Dale Long, still hitting a lofty .373.

But the steam started to escape, and the Pirates lost a few here and there. Pittsburgh fell out of the lead, regained it, and on June 18 fell back for good. The team that finally put the Pirates away was Milwaukee, getting ready to begin its brief dynasty as the league powerhouse. And who was managing Milwaukee? Fred Haney. Easygoing Fred Haney had moved to the Braves as a coach; later, Brave manager Charley Grimm was replaced, and

Haney was the man who replaced him. One seldom feels saddened by the firing of managers. It is less a firing than a game of musical chairs.

Once out of first, the remaining air escaped with a loud pop, and the team descended. The club lost eight straight late in June, as Dale Long went into a tailspin, going 0-for-21. Perhaps he was right; $25 fines worked more wonders than pay boosts. The team dropped into fourth place. But all the time, Roberto Clemente kept hitting. This was his second year. George Sisler had corrected one tendency, Clemente's head bob. But for all of Sisler's lectures on the virtues of the base on balls, Clemente kept right on swinging at everything in sight. "Hit only those pitches you like," Sisler warned Clemente. Clemente nodded soberly, and instead of walking 18 times as he had in 1955, Clemente walked five times fewer in 1956. And came to bat 70 more times. Clemente was hitting only those pitches he liked. He liked them all.

But he also hit them all, or nearly all. He would say later of those early seasons, "When I first came up, I tried to pull every pitch and hit it out of the park. Now I just try to meet the ball where it is pitched and hit between the fielders. I am happy to get singles and doubles and let the home runs come by themselves."

Obviously he wasn't trying to pull every ball in 1956. Line drives whistled to every field, and those Clemente ground balls—hit like buckshot—whipped past blinded infielders. The base hits mounted, if the bases on balls did not, and though Clemente could not maintain a .350 average—at least not this year—he stayed close to the league leaders.

And he got his occasional home run. On July 21, the Pirates faced Cincinnati and the hottest pitcher in baseball, burly Brooks Lawrence. Young Lawrence had won his first 13 games. For eight innings, he seemed on his way to Number 14. Then in the ninth, with the Pirates trailing 3–1, Lee Walls singled, Frank Thomas singled, and Roberto Clemente hit the second pitch into the right center-field bleachers for a three-run home run, and a 4–3 Pittsburgh victory. It was Clemente's fourth home run of the campaign, but when the brief jubilation of that day had ended, Pittsburgh still was 12 games out of first place, and headed down.

Clemente kept whaling away. On July 24, he drove in four runs, with a home run, a triple, and a sacrifice fly, in a 6–2 win over Chicago. And the next day he became news, in a game against the Cubs in Forbes Field. The Pirates had led by four runs until the Cubs got seven in the eighth, and going into the bottom of the ninth, Chicago was on top, 8–5. The Pirates quickly filled the bases with nobody out, and Clemente at bat. The Cubs called in a big bespectacled right-hander out of the bullpen, a man who would become more famous later for the way he wrote about baseball than the way he pitched it, though he pitched it quite well. His name was Jim Brosnan, and Brosnan made just one pitch.

Clemente belted it to the deepest part of the playing field of spacious Forbes Field, and three Pirate runners gleefully scampered home, to tie the score. Manager Bobby Bragan stood in the third-base coaching box, and as Clemente bore down on him, Bragan held up both hands to stop the fleet young Pirate. But Clemente ignored Bragan's sign, ignored the shout Bragan hurled at him, and kept on going, around third, and home, sliding in just ahead of the play, for an inside-the-park grandslam home-run and a 9–8 Pirate victory.

Bragan tells it this way:

"Phew! Here Clemente ties the game for sure, and I

throw up the stop sign. After all, we have some long ball hitters coming up, no one out, and getting Bobby home with the winning run looks easy. I hold up both hands and say, 'Stop!' but not Roberto. Roberto, he just keeps going, and of course he scored and we won. But it was a close play. Wow!"

And Clemente? What did he say? Once before he'd missed a sign, and it had cost him $25. Had he not seen Bragan put his hands up? Had he not heard Bragan's shrill 'Stop!'?

Of course he'd seen and heard Bragan. "I say to Bobby, 'Get out of my way,' and I score. Just like that. I think we have nothing to lose as we got the score tied without my run and if I score, the game is over and we don't have to play anymore tonight."

The reasoning was simple, if defective. Clemente felt the team had nothing to lose. The game was already tied. Why not risk it? Of course, with nobody out, coaches invariably hold up men at third on similar plays. Somebody is likely to get that run home.

Except for two things. This was Pittsburgh, where potential runs had a way of staying put, and dying. And anyway, this was Roberto Clemente, a man who does not enjoy breaking rules or disdaining managers' signs, but a man with a genius to sense when he can score on a close play and when he cannot. He sensed he would make it. He did, and the Pirates did not have to play anymore that night.

Sportswriters asked Bragan, probably facetiously, whether he intended to fine Clemente for deliberately ignoring his sign. Bragan smiled weakly and said, "Roberto is quite a player. He just likes to hit and run." He wasn't about to fine his grand-slammer.

Bragan was right. Clemente did like to hit and run. In

his last 170 times at bat, Clemente had not received a single base on balls. He also singled home a run that night, and in two days against Chicago, Clemente had hammered in nine runs.

No, you don't fine men who drive in nine runs in two days. Not that Bragan did not want to, some of the time. Bragan once told writer Stanley Frank a story that may well be apocryphal:

"I've often felt like using a ballplayer's head for fungo practice, and I came awful close to obeying that impulse last season [1956] in a game we lost by one run. Bob Clemente, the third best hitter in the league, went up there with two out and none on, and proceeded to end the game by getting thrown out tamely on a bunt.

" 'Bunting with nobody on base when we needed a run to tie was the dumbest play I've ever seen,' I raved. 'You must be loco to pull a boner like that. There was only one thing for you to do. You had to be up there, swinging for a home run.'

"Clemente looked me squarely in the eye and shrugged. 'Boss, me no feel like home run,' he said.

"Does anybody know an answer to that one?"

We can suggest an answer. Clemente played the percentages, just as Bragan would have wanted him to. Clemente hit exactly seven home runs in 1956 in 543 times at bat. That's over 75 at bats for every home run. The odds on Clemente hitting a home run every time he came up were over 75-to-1 against him. Even in the halcyon days of lively balls and lively bats, it is far easier to score a run other than by a home run. Clemente scored 66 runs in 1956 in those 543 at bats. A run every eight or nine times he batted. A run that began with a bunt base hit, a solid base hit, a rare walk, an error by the opposition, but seldom—very seldom—a run that stemmed from a home run. As I say, the story is probably apocryphal. Clemente, even in his very first days with the Pirates, did not speak the way Bragan and Stanley Frank have him talking. He did not say then, and he does not say today, "Me no feel like home run." Clemente does not speak the language of Tarzan of the Apes, and he resents being portrayed as such.

Still—as he would say at a later date—what does it matter which language a man speaks best? Judge him as a ballplayer, not a grammarian.

Bragan was closer to his man when he had said, "Roberto is quite a player. He just likes to hit and run."

But Clemente liked to do more. He loved to throw. In 1956 he picked up twenty assists in the outfield. He soon developed a pet play. When batters ripped singles to right field and made a too-wide turn around first, Clemente would whip the ball to Dale Long at first, behind the runner, and the base hit was suddenly evaporated into an out. It was not his only way of racking up the assists. He could fire line drives from the right-field fence to third base, and chop down runners trying to advance from first on a single. He could catch fly balls in medium right field, and throw out men coming down from third to the plate after the catch. To any base, and on any situation, he could and would throw his low-trajectory bullets, and over the years nobody in baseball has thrown much better.

But the Pirates floundered. Bobby Bragan tried a new tack on August 18, 1956. He shook up his batting order, placing pitcher Bob Friend in the number seven spot, and catcher Jack Shepard ninth. The Pirates responded by winning, 9–1, so for ten days Bragan tinkered with his batting order. Usually Bill Mazeroski found himself batting ninth. Yes, he later said ruefully, it embarrassed him to bat after the pitcher, and sometimes two notches after the pitcher. But the top of the order seemed equally zany. Frank Thomas, Bragan's biggest gun, a man who would hit 25 home runs and drive in 80 runs in 1956, became the Pirate lead-off. The next big slugger, Dale Long, batted second. Then came Virdon, Lee Walls, Clemente, and Groat. Perhaps it made sense. Perhaps it was Bragan's way of shaking up not only his batting order, but his batters. In any event, the Pirates went out and lost eight straight games, and on August 25, when they blew a five-run lead to the Cards, the team was 24 games out of first, down in sixth place, with a 51-and-72 record.

The losing streak ended the next day, when Clemente belted two doubles and Bob Friend pitched a shutout, as Pittsburgh beat Chicago, 2–0 and 2–1, in a Sunday double-header. But it was a brief respite. The team sagged further, and ended in seventh place. But not a bad seventh, just one game behind the sixth-place Giants. Bob Friend won 17 games in 1956, and led the league in innings pitched with 314, but he also lost 17, and young Vernon Law, who kept looking like a future winner, was not a present winner. Law posted an 8-and-16 mark. Ronnie Kline, a young fast-balling right-hander, won 14 games, but he lost 18, most in the league. Still, Kline was another workhorse; he hurled 264 innings, and his e.r.a. was a respectable 3.38.

But the team's stars were not pitchers. Bill Virdon, who'd come over from St. Louis, played in 157 games, most in the league, and he batted a rousing .319. Flanking Virdon was Roberto Clemente, just a hair behind with a .311 mark, in his second big league season. Clemente had 30 doubles in 1956, seven triples, and seven home runs. He drove in 60 runs and he stole seven bases. Injuries, as usual, had cut down his play, but Clemente got into 147 games. It would be the most games he'd play in one season until 1963.

Yet to Clemente it was not a terribly good season, precisely because the Pirates ended seventh. The Pirates figured very much in the pennant outcome. But even this ended bitterly.

On the next to last weekend, Pittsburgh entertained the Dodgers, as Brooklyn made a belated charge at league-leading Milwaukee. The Pirates slapped them down, winning three games out of four, and there was glee in the Pirate clubhouse those days. It always is fun to knock down a pennant contender, and more fun beating a team from the big city—New York. But on the last Saturday of the year, the Dodgers hosted Pittsburgh, and this time the Brooks won both ends of a doubleheader, while St. Louis was whipping Milwaukee's Warren Spahn. The next day the Dodgers again beat Pittsburgh, and glee turned to gloom. Brooklyn had won the pennant by beating Pittsburgh.

6

"My Tonsils Were Okay. It Was My Back That Hurt"

IN THE WINTER of 1956, Bob Clemente returned home a victor. In his sophomore year he had proved himself one of the better hitters of the National League. Before the 1957 season Clemente would receive in the mail a new contract from his Pittsburgh bosses, offering him a healthy increase.

During the same hiatus, Clemente generously dipped into his earnings, and bought his mother and father a new home. He spent $12,500, back in the winter of 1956, a startling figure for a house in Puerto Rico, where property values were not then, nor are they today, as inflated as in the States.

So there was a sense of conquering hero in this return of the native. But Clemente actually knew better. His back, never good the past years, had steadily become worse. A full season of play, and then a winter of ball in the Caribbean, hacked away at the muscles and nerves of the sore back. There would be other injuries and illnesses at other times, but few so persistent and enervating as

Clemente's weak back. He would miss over 40 games in 1957 because of the back, and even when he would play, wrapped in braces, he lacked his usual power, speed, and agility. It became painful to bend for base hits, sheer torment to slide. His swing was restricted, and for a joyous swinger like Clemente, this was like swinging in a phone booth, living in a strait jacket.

Still, he had endured the back through 1956, and in 1956 he played 147 games. Perhaps rest would keep the back under control; perhaps it would get better.

It got worse. Early in spring training at Fort Myers, Clemente wrenched the back, and he began to sit out exhibition games. The 1956 Pirates had fooled a lot of people. Not because they had finished a bare game behind the New York Giants, but because for nine days they had actually led the league. No longer did the remainder of the circuit treat the Pirates with contempt. The respect deepened during spring training. The Pirates chewed up their exhibition foes, ending with a 20-and-10 record.

Part of the respect had little to do with wins and losses, either in the spring of 1957 or the past summer of 1956. It stemmed from a growing realization that the Pirate right fielder was something special, a young man who could hit, run, field, and throw, and do all of these not only superlatively well, but with a brimming confidence, with the verve of a man who knew what he was doing.

What he was doing, on opening day of 1957, was sitting miserably in the dugout, bent in discomfort. His back, carefully nursed the last days of the spring program, had not come around. And a second aspect of Clemente's career had begun. Men who swing a bat as well as Clemente, who throw like a howitzer and run like the wind, find it difficult to come by sympathy.

"Clemente's sick?" someone will say. "I wish *I* was as sick."

Others said less kind things, then and more recently. *Crybaby* was one of the words used. *Hypochondriac*, another. *Goldbrick*. Soon a reputation grew. Clemente was not a man who could stand the slightest pain or distress (they said); he was a man who magnified his ills (if he had any to magnify), a man who definitely had not come to play, they said.

So the Pirate lineup on opening day—a damp, dreary, dark April afternoon at Forbes Field—went this way:

Lee Walls, lf
Roman Mejias, rf
Dale Long, 1b
Frank Thomas, 3b
Bill Virdon, cf
Dick Groat, ss
Bill Mazeroski, 2b
Bob Friend, p
Hank Foiles, c

Yes, that's right. Pitcher Friend batted eighth and catcher Foiles ninth.

On that opening day, without Clemente, the Pirates blasted the Giants, and Johnny Antonelli, winning 9–2. It was, for all the rain, a gala opening, and 33,405 fans loved every moist minute.

Rain wiped out other games the first week, and on April 20, when the Pirate record was 1-and-1, Clemente made his first appearance. He played right field and led off, but Johnny Podres, of Brooklyn, shackled Clemente and his mates as well, and the Dodgers won, 2–0. Clemente had a three-hit ball game in the opening game of a doubleheader the next day, helping to beat Brooklyn, 6–3, but in the nightcap he went hitless, and Pittsburgh lost, 7–4.

After 13 games, Bob was batting .310. But Clemente had knocked in just three runs. True, he had hit a home run, again off Brooks Lawrence, but other than that, he did not look right at the plate. Still, there weren't many observers to notice. The Pirates suddenly had hitters all over. Hank Foiles, the fleet catcher who had batted ninth on opening day, was ripping the ball at a .362 clip. Close behind came shortstop Dick Groat, hitting .325. Bob Skinner, in left field, had started to hit, with power. Dale Long had not come up to his 1956 form, so the Pirates quickly swapped him to Chicago for Dee Fondy. Fondy began to spray line drives all over the league, and Pirate fans forgot about Long and his year-old heroics. Frank Thomas, no matter whether he played third, first, or the outfield, wielded a big bat.

So Clemente was not hitting for power, and very soon not hitting at all? Who cared?

Bobby Bragan cared, for one. Bragan had known in 1956 his league-leading team wasn't as good as all that; he'd settled for fifth place. And Bragan knew the name of of the game is pitching. He knew it then; he surely knew it years later when he managed the powerful Braves, but could not win a pennant because the Braves did not have the pitching. He would need every bat—now—and he counted on Clemente's, to offset his lack of pitching.

The Pirate pitchers were Bob Friend, an established star; Vernon Law, always promising but in those days never fulfilling; young Kline, who somehow lost more games than his skills seemed to indicate he should; and reliever ElRoy Face, not yet the stopper he would become.

With all the .300 hitters, Pittsburgh slipped into last place, behind Chicago. Bragan had been hired to inject spirit. All right, he had done just that. But enthusiasm seldom hits a ball over a fence, or strikes out a man, or starts a double play. The flesh has to be there, too.

The Pirates lost seven straight in mid-May, and in the sixth of those losses, Bob Friend—the team's ace—gave up six runs in the first inning. It marked another of Clemente's rare good days at the plate. First man up in the first inning, he hit an inside-the-park home run, and later he belted a triple and a single. Actually, Clemente must have been feeling better; five days later he hit another home run, his third of the year, and this time the blow beat Milwaukee and Juan Pizarro, 2–1. But not too much better; he did not hit another home run for a month, and this one—number four—would be his last of the year.

Soon Pittsburgh was 8-and-21, and Bobby Bragan started to run out of time. Never a man to take defeat quietly, Bragan was baiting umpires even more than was his usual fashion. But he had other trouble. When the Pirates lost their seventh straight, to Philadelphia, in the first half of a doubleheader on May 12 at Forbes Field, Bragan revamped his lineup for the second contest. He benched Frank Thomas, though Thomas had two hits in the opener.

Thomas burned. On May 13 he went to Forbes Field hoping to thrash out his discomfiture with Bragan. He couldn't find Bragan, and because he was still burning, he sounded off to a Pirate front-office bigwig at the ball park, and later collared Joe L. Brown in the lobby of the Knickerbocker Hotel in Chicago, on May 14.

That afternoon, Bragan assembled his squad before the game, and allowed that he was burning, too:

"I play to win and I try to play my best men. If I thought Johnny O'Brien could beat the Cubs today instead of Ron Kline, I'd pitch O'Brien. I'm the manager and it's up to me to make the decision. I don't take orders from anybody: John Galbreath [president], Tom Johnson [vice-president], or Joe Brown. If you fellows have any complaints at all, I want you to register them with me, not the front office. Do you understand that, Frank Thomas?"

Thomas said he understood, and went out on the field where he had his best afternoon of 1957, with a single, two doubles, and a home run.

But Bragan remained unhappy. On May 24, while directing a losing game to Philadelphia, Bragan was ejected. Bragan's players did not react well, and ten players and a coach joined Bragan in the shower. It was not the last of Bragan's ejections. He had reason for churlishness, other than his team's dismal showing or Frank Thomas's burn. Odd injuries plagued the club. Dee Fondy, the league's leading hitter at the time, was having a catch in the bullpen with ElRoy Face one day in June. A fan yelled to Fondy, the first baseman looked up, and Face threw the ball; the result was two broken bones in Fondy's face. A relief pitcher was struck on the head by an errant throw—from another Pirate. Dick Hall, the six-foot six-inch outfielder, now transplanted to the pitching mound, came down with a sore arm.

An error by Clemente lost a ball game in the 11th inning of a game on June 9. Milwaukee batter Frank Torre, older brother of today's star catcher, Joe, lined a single to right, and Clemente bent for the ball. It slithered away for an extra base, and a moment later the runner scored on another single. Clemente did not offer an alibi, but bending for base hits was torture. Clemente sat out the second game that day, returned to the lineup the next day (and went 0-for-4), did not play the next day, and that is the way it went: missing every other game, sometimes two or three in a row. When the team had played 90 games, Clemente had played just 57.

The back kicked up at unfortunate moments. Clemente ripped three hits in four times to the plate on June 17, in the opener of a doubleheader, and then in his first lick in the second contest, swung and connected for another hit, but in the process threw his back out and had to leave the game.

The Pirates, reasonably worried about their right fielder but not sure his trouble lay in his back, suggested he have his tonsils out. Clemente consented, and sat out a few more games while recuperating. The Pirates announced rosily, "Now you'll feel better," to which Clemente replied, "My tonsils were okay. It is my back that hurts." He went to St. Louis to see a chiropractor, but the pain kept returning.

All this must have nagged at Bragan. Late in June the team faced the Cincinnati Reds, and Cincinnati's pitcher, Raul Sanchez, seemed to be dampening the ball somewhat more than most pitchers. Bragan complained but got nowhere, so the peppy manager instructed two Pirates to carry a bucket of water onto the field. "Here," one Pirate shouted. "You want to wet the ball? Here." An umpire weariedly ejected Bragan, and league president Warren Giles fined Bobby $50. This made the total $135 Bragan had been fined in his four ejections. The worst was yet to happen.

June faded into a sweltering July, but Clemente's bat stayed cool. He labored through a 15-inning contest, going 1-for-7, and in a stretch of four games was just 2-for-17. His batting average sank below .250. Meanwhile, Groat was slapping hits to every field and batting .335, third best in the league; Bob Skinner ranked fourth, at .333; Dee Fondy stood fifth, with .324; and Frank Thomas, at .312, was the league's eighth best. Hank Foiles had dipped some, but was still hitting .297, and young Mazeroski pleasantly fooled everyone who thought of him as a good-field, no-hit infielder, batting .287. Gene Freese, Bill Virdon, and Gene Baker all were outhitting Clemente by over twenty points.

Still, Pittsburgh was last or next to last through the first half of the season, and on Wednesday night, July 31, during a 4–2 loss to Milwaukee, Bragan received his fifth ejection of the season. Bragan disputed a decision at second base by umpire Stan Landes. His form of disputation was the classic thumb to the nose, four fingers erect and wagging. But the aftermath was more than the ejection. Bragan wandered into the dugout, and then came out onto the field carrying a bottle of orange pop. Courteously, he offered a sip to plate umpire Frank Dascoli. Dascoli abruptly refused. Undismayed, Bragan went to each of the umpires—even to Landes—offering orange pop. Enraged, the umpires shooed Bragan off the premises, Warren Giles came down with a $100 fine, and on August 3 a harassed Joe L. Brown announced he had fired Bragan "for the good of the team."

Who would be the new manager?

Well, the job was offered to coach Clyde Sukeforth—the Pirate who had first been enthralled by Bob Clemente in a Montreal uniform—but Sukey studied the standings, his team roster, and the tenure of past managers, and said No, thanks.

So Brown asked Danny Murtaugh, a square-jawed, blue-eyed tobacco-chewing Irishman, and Murtaugh narrowed those blue eyes and thought for a minute before he spat out a spray of brown juice. "Sure," he said. What did he have to lose, besides his composure, his digestion, and—

naturally—the job? Nor was anybody fooling Murtaugh. Brown's announcement to the press made it clear that Murtaugh was an "interim" appointment. He would finish the season, and then it would be decided just who the manager was.

Actually, Murtaugh had little to lose. The club was seventh the day he was hired. It promptly lost a doubleheader to Chicago, and plunged into the cellar. Murtaugh could only go up, or out.

Murtaugh did not go up very much. He and the Pirates ended the year of 1957 in a tie with Chicago for seventh place, which means a tie for seventh and eighth places. Not much improvement, you say? You say wrong. From the date of Murtaugh's hiring, the Pirates played .500 ball to the season's end. Unfortunately, Chicago played about as well, so the two ended with 62 wins and 92 losses, but Murtaugh, the interim man hired to mark time until Brown had scoured the baseball world for an established hand, had served notice his hand was as good as anybody's.

The change from Bragan to Murtaugh did not affect Clemente. His bat remained inert. Not that Murtaugh actually was much change. He too represented the spirit of the game, a man who got caught up in the action and viewed it as a boy might, on a sandlot nine. Murtaugh knew his baseball, but he never pretended to be a raging intellectual, nor did he pretend to be a button-down collar type, a manager you find not in the bush leagues sweating out bus rides with his boys but rather in the ad agencies of Madison Avenue. Murtaugh was certainly not Madison Avenue. Third Avenue, maybe, before they tore down the El tracks.

Clemente had another infrequent three-hit game on August 14, two singles and a double, in a 10–3 win over

Philadelphia, but Pittsburgh remained last. Four days later, Clemente celebrated his twenty-third birthday, against Brooklyn, and he had two doubles, but he had them over the course of a doubleheader, and he ended the day 2-for-8.

It became increasingly harder to notice Clemente, and it might have been tough enough had he been ripping line drives all summer. For this was the summer of the big change, the year both the New York Giants and the Brooklyn Dodgers tore up their roots and announced their intention to move west. The Giants had played baseball in the Polo Grounds, on the banks of the Harlem River, ever since the days of the 1880s, when mustachioed Jim Mutrie, in his black stovepipe hat, shouted to his New York club, "C'mon, you Giants!" and gave them their nickname. Few teams ever seemed closer to their home park than the Giants did to the Polo Grounds. It seemed impossible to imagine them anywhere else. Where would the ghosts of Mathewson and Iron Man McGinnity, Ross Young and Mel Ott find peace, except in the horseshoe-shaped Polo Grounds, with its odd close-in fences at the foul poles and its extravagant expanse of grass in deep center field? It had been an old, creaking park for years—nay, for decades—with pillars obstructing spectators' views, a park without adequate space for automobiles, a park with a tiny bleachers section out beyond center field, over 500 feet from the plate, yet a park with many of the wisest, most loyal fans ever to cling to a team's rises and falls. Now they were to be fans without a team, for the Giants announced on August 19, 1957, that next year they'd be the San Francisco Giants.

And the Dodgers. Imagine the Dodgers out of Ebbets Field, playing someplace other than in the wonderful, zany, rich, odd, exciting, mad borough of Brooklyn. It couldn't be done. If the Giant fans were fiercely loyal, the Dodger fans were willing to kill, or to die, for their team. If any team's followers deserved an unbroken lease, it would have been those Dodger fans at Ebbets Field. The Giant fans had stopped coming to the ball park through the years of the 1940s and 1950s, as the Giants sagged lower and lower in the standings. But the Dodger fans stormed down the doors to see their beloved Bums. No team had ever made more money than had the Dodgers the five years prior to 1957. Yet it was in 1957 that Walter O'Malley made it known the club would move to the West Coast, and would then be not the Brooklyn Dodgers, but the Los Angeles Dodgers. From Bums to Angels. It seemed ludicrous, unbelievable, insane. And imminent.

The Pirates had an odd honor that season. They were on the road the last part of September as the season drew to a close, and they played in Ebbets Field on September 24—the last game played in the park—just as they would five days later play in the last game ever by the New York Giants at the Polo Grounds. Clemente did not do much in the Ebbets Field finale as Brooklyn won, 2–0. In the Giants' New York swan song, attended by 11,606 diehards on a day the sun tried valiantly to break through a yellow sky, Clemente had three hits and scored three runs. The Pirates won that last game in the Polo Grounds, 9–1, but once again nobody seemed to be noticing. It was a game marked by sentiment; fans cheered when Willie Mays batted, and when Bobby Thomson batted, and they hung out signs, STAY, TEAM, STAY. When the game was over, the fans stormed onto the playing field, racing past a handful of policemen who did not try to stop them, and for a half hour or so engaged in trivial vandalism. They ripped up dirt from the infield, uprooted home plate, tore down the fences, carried off washroom signs.

An era ended. Baseball, in the National League, left New York, not to return until the Mets and Casey Stengel came swaggering and staggering along in 1962.

To Pittsburgh, the last game counted more than just a footnote to baseball history. By beating the Giants that day and the day before, Pittsburgh managed to keep out of the cellar. Just barely. The club ended tied with Chicago, and Bob Clemente went home, if not a happy young man, at least not a member of an undisputed tail-ender.

Definitely not a happy young man. Clemente played in 111 games that season, and he batted a lowly .253. Never had he batted so poorly. Never had he knocked in so few runs—30. Never had he failed to steal a single base in a full season of play.

7

"I Heard It Crack"

ROBERTO CLEMENTE did not spend his usual winter after the 1957 season had ended. Instead of going home to Puerto Rico for another go at winter-league baseball, Clemente went back for a brief rest, and returned to the States.

He had a date. With the Marines.

For six months, Clemente fulfilled his obligation to the country of his citizenship—the United States of America—by training at Parris Island Marine Corps Recruit Depot, in South Carolina.

It is said the Marines will make a man out of a boy. Roberto Clemente has insisted he has been a man ever since the age of seventeen, when he put away his schoolbooks to enter a full-fledged profession.

Still, the Marines nearly always leave their particular mark on those men or boys who pass through the Corps. Roberto Clemente is no exception. He went into the Corps with an aching back. He came out a reasonably well man.

When he is asked how this extraordinary change occurred (men with strong sacroiliac-lumbar regions go into service and often come out with the famous "aching backs," but seldom does it work the other way), Clemente answers tersely:

"I worked like hell."

That sums it up. A Marine recruit works long hours on arduous tasks. Clemente threw himself into the routine. The rhythm of the work smoothed out the crazy-jig spasms that for so long had seized his back ever since the day he picked up a too-light bat and swung it too hard.

When Roberto Clemente reported to the Pirate camp at Fort Myers, he was a different man. Which is not to say he would always be well again. That still is another person. Clemente had licked his back trouble, at least for a spell. His stomach, his head, his arm—those are other stories; their telling would turn this book into a ten-year run of *Ben Casey*.

The sight of a once-again strong-backed Roberto Clemente meant more than just a healthier right fielder. Players reacted positively to the new Clemente. The whole team took on a healthier air. Not since 1949 had a Pirate club finished better than last or next to last, and that Pittsburgh team of nine years ago ended sixth. Not in a decade had a Pirate team finished in the first division. No team in National League history had been so perennially a tail-ender as the Pirates of the past quarter century.

Now Roberto Clemente swirled across the field, charging line drives. Now he pirouetted in the batter's box, chasing bad pitches and hitting them with that characteristic crunch. Now he whirled and flashed, and threw rifle shots to distant bases. And in the wake of his dance, his teammates caught the beat.

Some men did not have to be led. Bob Friend had for the past several years demonstrated his pitching skill. He'd led the league in innings pitched the past two seasons, and in earned-run average the year before that. Frank Thomas, playing wherever they put him, continued to hit home runs and knock in runs. In the five preceding years he'd hit 126 home runs and batted in 437 runs. They called Bill Mazeroski "No touch" because his hands moved so swiftly you seldom saw him pick up ground balls before he had already thrown them to first. He would, they said, never wear out a glove. And now he'd begun to hit. In 1957 he'd belted a solid .283. Catcher Hank Foiles had come along so quickly he'd made the 1957 All Star squad (and in his one turn at bat, he singled). In 1957 Dick Groat hit a soaring .315, better than any infielder in the league—better than Ernie Banks, Al Dark, Eddie Mathews, Ken Boyer, Joe Adcock.

To these, add such names as Vernon Law, ElRoy Face, and Bill Virdon, and such promising rookie pitchers as George Witt, a sunburned redheaded youngster from Long Beach, California (drafted, like Clemente, from the Dodger organization), and Curt Raydon, another free-flinging stringbean right-hander, and you could smell the revolution that began to stir in the second division as 1958 unfolded its opening day flags.

What a race those silken colors presaged! The Giants, newly nestled in Seals Stadium, San Francisco, and bristling with powerful young rookies, plus a red-hot Willie Mays, tore up the league the opening weeks. But they could not shake Milwaukee and its pitching duo of Warren Spahn and Lou Burdette, plus more great young hurlers, Joey Jay, Carlton Willey, and Juan Pizarro. The Dodgers faltered in their new home, and the Pirates and the lowly Cubs came on. Why not the Cubs? Ernie Banks would whiplash 47 home runs, to lead both leagues. The teams played musical chairs as they fought for the lead. On July

4, Milwaukee had edged ahead of San Francisco, but exactly seven games separated the first-place Braves and the last-place Dodgers, closest first half of a pennant race in league history.

In a race like that, turnstiles spun like ballet dancers. Pittsburgh claimed its share of those merry turnstiles. The year before, 850,732 fans paid their way into Forbes Field. Now with Frank Thomas belting home runs at his best pace ever, with Bob Skinner among the league leaders all season, with Bob Friend winning far more games than he'd ever won, with young Red Witt and Curt Raydon knocking off 17 wins between them (and losing just six), and with a healthy Bob Clemente hitting, running, catching, and throwing—well, ancient Forbes Field itself seemed to spin giddily. A year before, the Pirates fought to stay out of the cellar, and barely won the fight. Now they fought for a high perch in a pennant race nobody would give up on. And instead of 850,000 fans, the year would bring in more than 1,310,000. Five teams drew over a million fans. The league had the second best year at the box office in its long history.

Danny Murtaugh managed the team with dash and daring enough to make Bobby Bragan quickly forgotten, and with skill enough to make Fred Haney just as forgotten. Murtaugh had a habit of hazing rookies. It does not sound funny in print, and it surely flouts etiquette. Murtaugh enjoyed spitting tobacco juice at a newcomer's spikes. It was his way of saying, "Welcome to the club, and be on your toes."

The club was on its toes, and it trampled on the toes of six other clubs. When the season was over, Pittsburgh—yes, Pittsburgh—had finished second. Pittsburgh had clawed its way up from a tie for the cellar to the second spot on the ladder. Just Milwaukee lay ahead, and Milwaukee was the defending world champion.

That was the year that was, in one big swallow. It got there in tiny sips.

At spring training, though the team seemed friskier, you couldn't always prove it in the standings, or at the dispensary. For a spell, the Pirates had the worst won-lost record of all National League teams in Florida. And frisky though it was, the club had its physical woes. Ted Kluszewski, the first baseman over from Cincinnati, had a lame back, and not until the last weekend of spring training could big Klu play a full nine-inning game. Bob Friend, who had suffered through an abscessed throat in 1957, had a pitching arm that kept tightening up on him. Friend was one Pirate who arrived in training camp every year looking not the slightest bit rested. Each year, from 1949 through 1957, Friend went back to college, putting in a semester of study for eight straight years, until he had received his bachelor of science degree in economics from the University of Purdue. Each spring, Bob Friend was a worn young man when he would start to get ready for the grueling year ahead. (And each summer he'd pitch as many innings as anybody in the league.) On top of it all, Friend—those first years—was a fidgety youngster, a man who burned energy even when he was sitting still, or trying to. They called him Nervous Nervous Friend those years. And now he had a sore arm.

Just before spring training closed, Bill Mazeroski hurt himself. Not badly, but enough that he would be kept out of the opening day batting order on April 15.

There were bright spots. On April 6, 1958, Bob Clemente's grand-slam home run whipped Kansas City, 5–2. Vernon Law went the distance that day. The day before, sore-armed Bob Friend had gone the full nine, so *that* problem seemed to be easing. And on April 7—third day in a row—another Pirate, Ron Kline, pitched a complete game, setting down the Boston Red Sox, 4–2, as Frank Thomas hit his fifth home run of the practice season. With this win, the Pirates escaped from the Grapefruit League cellar, and Philadelphia fell in.

This was to be a wingding year, 1958. You could smell it shaping up. On April 9, Cincinnati's feared slugger, Frank Robinson, was struck with a pitched ball thrown by Washington's Camilo Pascual, and had to be hustled to a hospital. When they start beaning the boys in spring training, you know there are fireworks ahead.

The next day Pittsburgh ran smack into the fireworks. Literally. The Pirates traveled to Mexico to play the Mexico City Red Devils, and 30,000 fans—that's not a misprint—came out to see the big leaguers play the hometown boys. The ball park was a sea of sound, and as the Pirates mercilessly chopped up the Red Devils, the fans became—shall we say?—impatient. Bob Friend held the Mexico City hitters scoreless for six innings, and Bob Clemente hit a home run, and to show their—shall we say?—deviltry, the fans in the second tier showered flaming newspapers and beer cans down on the playing field. The final score was 10–2, and the Pirates ran off the singed field, their ears ringing.

The club finally split two games with their farm team in Columbus, and in the Pirate win, 15–2, Frank Thomas belted two home runs, one a grand slam, and knocked in six runs.

So the team acted ready.

They acted readier opening day, April 15, at Milwaukee's County Stadium, as they battled the Braves for 14 spine-tingling innings, winning 4–3 as young Ron Blackburn held the Braves to one hit in three innings of relief. Clemente had two singles and a double in six trips, as 43,339 fans watched the defending champions lose.

Clemente had a triple and a single the next day, but Lou Burdette was too much, and suddenly the good look turned ill. The Pirates could not win for losing; Bob Clemente could not buy a hit. In the field, Pittsburgh began to make errors—five in one contest against Cincinnati on April 19, three by Dick Groat. Still, in the field they also provided the rare thrills. In the fifth inning of a contest at Forbes Field on April 22, Milwaukee's Del Rice doubled with one out, and pitcher Bob Buhl lined a drive to deepest left center. Fleet Bill Virdon turned his back and raced for the ball. At the last moment he dove, one-handed the ball, and though he fell heavily on his shoulder, he held the baseball. The next hitter, Red Schoendienst, shot a hot line drive to right field, where Bob Clemente speared the ball and rifled a patented throw to Dick Groat at second base, to double off Del Rice. But Hank Aaron hit a three-run home run, and Milwaukee triumphed, 5–2.

As April ended, Clemente caught fire, and so did the Pirates. He stole a base on April 24—something he hadn't done all of 1957—and he had two base hits as the Pirates beat Philadelphia, 7–4. The next day he had a hand in every run as the Pirates whipped Cincinnati, 4–3. In the sixth, Clemente doubled and eventually scored on Hank Foiles' sacrifice fly. In the eighth he poled a three-run home run off Harvey Haddix, and by the end of the day his three hits in five at bats had moved him to .378, eighth best in the league.

He had three more hits the next day in an 8–4 win over Cincinnati, and then two hits at the Los Angeles Coliseum, as the Pirates visited Walter O'Malley's cow pasture for the first time. Bob Friend won his third straight ball game, and when the first month ended, the Pirates were a game out of first place. Clemente was hitting .400.

On April 30, however, Bob Clemente made a quick throw in a game against the Dodgers, and felt a sharp twinge in his arm. And a new chapter in the life of Battered Bob Clemente began to unfold. A year later, Clemente recounted the history of his (still) sore arm. "I heard it crack when I made a fast sidearm throw in 1958. It feels like needles in there, so I don't throw hard until I have to." The arm, he said, "hung down to the ground."

He sat out the game of May 1, and two days later, Bob Friend had to retire in the seventh inning of a game he was winning, 3–1, when his right arm tightened up on him.

But the Pirates kept right on winging away. Roman Mejias replaced Clemente, and it looked a bit like the time Lou Gehrig replaced Wally Pipp. Mejias went up to San Francisco, and in friendly Seals Stadium, where the wind was blowing out, Mejias blasted three home runs in the first game of a doubleheader. *That's* a second-stringer?

But Clemente was back the next day, as the Giants and Pirates played a wild game. For a few innings it was a contest; then the Pirates scored five runs in the seventh inning and three in the ninth, and going into the last of the ninth, the score was 11–1. But this Giant team had its spirit, too. They started to hit the ball long and short; baseballs flew over the fence or dribbled past straining infielders. And the runs piled up. Nine of them. Finally, with the score 11–10, the bases loaded, and two out, rookie Don Taussig lofted a short fly to right center field. Clemente, Dick Groat, and Bill Virdon converged gingerly on the ball as it drifted in the moist breeze, and Giant runners tore around the bases. Finally Bill Mazeroski burst through the uncertain caucus and clutched the pop fly before it fell to earth. The Pirates had won, but the scene was set for more furious days with the Giants before the year was out. In the fifth inning of that game, Giant right-hander Ruben Gomez had struck catcher Hank Foiles on the elbow with a pitch, and Foiles left the game. The Pirates did not quickly forget. Two days later, as Bob Friend came back to test his arm and was beaten by the Giants, matters came to a head. Lots of heads. Ron Blackburn hit Willie Kirkland with a pitch, and later Curt Raydon, a six-foot four-inch beanpole with obvious "control" problems, brushed back Eddie Bressoud, Willie Mays, Orlando Cepeda, and Willie Kirkland. And the Giant pitchers took their potshots back at Pirate hitters.

The Pirates left town—undoubtedly in haste—and again began winning. Vernon Law won his fourth, against one defeat; castoff Bob Porterfield hurled an 11-inning shutout in his first start as a Pirate, besting Curt Simmons; and Bob Friend also beat Philadelphia. In the three-game sweep, Clemente had five hits in eleven trips, three for extra bases.

The Pirates won their fifth in a row on May 13 as they whipped Cincinnati, 6–3. Meanwhile, the big men of the league had big days. Willie Mays had a look at O'Malley's short left-field wall, and beat a deadly tattoo against and over it, with consecutive home runs in the first and second innings, two triples, a single, and a base on balls, as the Giants belted Los Angeles, 16–9. Out in Chicago, Stan Musial came off the bench to pinch-hit a double down the left-field line off Moe Drabowsky. It was Musial's 3,000th major league hit, and the Cards won their sixth in a row.

Pittsburgh also made it six straight the next day, but streaks run both ways, and Pittsburgh dropped five ball games in a row, during which Ted Kluszewski's back trouble recurred and Clemente had to sit out a ball game because *his* back kicked up. Tell that to the Marines! (The ailments were not exclusively the players'. Hal Dixon, a National League umpire, got caught up in the fierceness of the action, and developed a bleeding ulcer. Yes, baseball is a sport, but the tensions can strangle the heartiest men.) Hank Foiles, back in action after being hit by that Ruben Gomez pitch, now chased a foul fly on May 23 and tripped over a roll of tarpaulin. He landed on his chin; 21 stitches sewed it together.

Meanwhile, Bob Friend, the tired grad, continued to win games as though he never had a sore arm in his life. On May 24 he won his seventh, and the next day the Giants were in town for a doubleheader. Just two quiet games of mayhem.

In the first game, Ruben Gomez got off to a quick lead. In the fourth inning Bill Mazeroski unpeeled a tremendous drive to left field, but it drifted foul. On the next pitch Gomez fired a fast ball, high and tight. The ball struck Maz's left arm. From the dugout came angry growls, and when Gomez batted in the fifth inning, Vernon Law—a deacon of his Mormon church—decked Gomez, and umpire Frank Dascoli strode to the mound to warn Law about beanballs. From the Pirate dugout bounded manager Murtaugh. He rushed at Gomez, who still held his bat, and suddenly players swarmed over the field in what appeared to be the beginning of war. Orlando Cepeda, the big Giant first baseman and a personal friend of Gomez's, headed for the Pirate mass. But before he could get there, teammate Willie Mays dropped Orlando with a flying tackle. The air escaped from the ready-to-pop balloon. Order was restored. The Giants won both games, 5–2 and 6–1. Murtaugh and Gomez each were fined $100. Fans from Fort Myers quickly rallied together and wired $100 to Murtaugh. During all the fuss, Bob

Clemente quietly had himself three hits in eight trips, one a triple.

By June 1 Milwaukee had grabbed the lead, with the Giants a game behind and Pittsburgh four back of the Giants. Los Angeles, in last place, was just ten games out of first. It got tighter.

Clemente—as streaky as his team—went into another slump. He has said, in recent years, that a slump is a product of one thing only—physical fatigue. It would seem that mental fatigue, nervous fatigue, is surely as potent a reason. But Clemente did have physical reason for his slump; his arm ached him. He began to sit out an occasional game, sometimes making a late-inning pinch-hitting appearance, or a running effort. By the end of the first week in June, Pittsburgh had lost 17 of its last 22 games, and Clemente had drifted down to a .286 batting mark. Moe Drabowsky hurled a one-hitter against Pittsburgh, the only hit an infield single, and after 50 games the Pirates now stood sixth, with a 24-and-26 record.

But those two right-handed rookies, George Witt and Curt Raydon, would change that all around. For this is the beauty of baseball. A team stumbles and sags, and the obituary writers nod their heads and say sagely, "Well, they've had it. Bunch of bums. I could have told you so." And along comes an unknown kid out of the bushes or an overage castoff from the other league, or maybe a sore-armed pitcher suddenly finds he can get men out with junk instead of a no-longer smoking fast ball, and the corpse is revived. Champions fall; unknowns swiftly take their place.

The Pirates knocked the Giants out of first place on June 11, as an established star, Frank Thomas, celebrating his twenty-ninth birthday, had one of his great days, two home runs and seven runs batted in. Another star,

Roberto Clemente, had three hits in five at bats, and the final score was 14–6. The next day it was a different game, a pitcher's game, as young nearly unknown Curt Raydon threw a two-hitter at the potent Giants, edging San Francisco, 2–1. A few days later, just as little known Red Witt, recalled from Columbus, pitched a complete game, beating Los Angeles, 2–1, and the man he outpitched was Sandy Koufax.

So it went, into the summer of 1958, as eight teams yes, eight—stayed within clutching distance of first place. Milwaukee and San Francisco looked like the teams to beat, but other teams kept beating them, and the big hitters, like Mays and Musial, both of whom had flirted with .500 averages, now found themselves benched. Mays, in fact, went to the hospital, so suspicious were the Giants that something physical ailed their slugger. Nothing did ail him, other than fatigue. In the tension that grew and swelled until it caught at a man's throat—the famous "choking up" which ballplayers consider the worst insult leveled against them, as though they were immune from emotional upsets—manager Murtaugh found himself arguing more and winning less. He was ejected by umpires for the fourth time that season, and the season was less than half over. The club could not untrack itself those middle weeks, and soon it dropped its seventh in a row, as Moe Drabowsky, rapidly becoming a Pirate killer, beat Pittsburgh, 3–1, on the eve of Drabowsky's wedding. Pittsburgh now lay sixth, just a half game out of the cellar, where Los Angeles resided. But the astonishing part of it is that the Pirates, losing streak and all, sixth place and all, were just five and a half games out of first place.

By July 4 things were no better, no worse, except that Bob Clemente went 1-for-7 in a double loss in Cincinnati, and was hitting .277.

From an unlikely source help came. In the minor leagues the past few seasons, a raw slugger named Dick Stuart had begun to make a name for himself. Two names. One, he sure could hit home runs, 66 of them in one year at Lincoln in the Western League. Two, he sure couldn't field very well. Stuart also had a flair for saying what lay on his tongue without letting his mind get in the way. But no matter how you sliced it, his home-run hitting wasn't baloney. On July 10, Dick Stuart joined the club, and promptly belted two of his specialties his first two days with Pittsburgh, one a grand-slammer. And the Pirates loosened up again. Not totally. Gene Baker, their fine all-round infielder, ruptured a knee ligament on July 13, and went under the knife. He would never be the same again.

The team won a few and lost a few, but it won more than it lost. On July 23 Pittsburgh beat Los Angeles twice, 11–3 and 6–3, as Clemente had a home run and four runs driven in in the first, and a double in the second. All the excitement, of course, wasn't restricted to the National League. Tension clutches both leagues, and all men. Ted Williams spat in the direction of fans on July 23, and was fined $250.

But our story is Pittsburgh, and Bob Clemente. Young Raydon beat his favorite clay pigeons, San Francisco, 10–0, as Clemente had a triple and a single, and two runs batted in. But the big gun those weeks was Frank Thomas. Thomas burst loose with a 15-game hitting streak. Pittsburgh won four straight before John Antonelli blanked them, 1–0 (as Clemente had two hits in three tries), and the Pirates stayed if not hot, at least quite warm. They won nine of eleven games, and Clemente rose up from below .275 toward .290. But mainly—now—it was the pitching that did it, as it nearly always is when a team wins regularly.

Kline blanked the Cards on August 1 (with Musial benched), tossing a four-hitter. The next day Clemente had three hits, and Vernon Law blanked the Cards again, in less than two hours. In a doubleheader the next day, Bob Friend shut out St. Louis, 2–0, and after five innings of the second game, when the game was halted by Pennsylvania's curfew law, Red Witt led the Cards, 2–0. Pittsburgh's pitchers had tossed 32 consecutive innings of shutout ball. And Pittsburgh had cozied into third place, just two games behind San Francisco.

The next day a ninth-inning home run by Clemente broke a 3–3 tie against Milwaukee, as Curt Raydon beat Juan Pizarro. Frank Thomas's bat cooled, so Clemente's hot hand was welcome, but the big guy now was Bob Skinner, the lanky left-handed left fielder hitting .330, fifth best in the league.

On August 8, Red Witt—no longer unknown—beat Cincinnati, 1–0, striking out ten. Clemente drove in the only run with a single in the sixth frame. Curt Raydon beat Cincy the next day, and then Pittsburgh won a fierce doubleheader the next day, 3–2 in ten innings, and 4–3. Clemente had two hits the first game, and rested the second. Pittsburgh now stood a half game behind San Francisco.

By this time, the Pirate fans felt it was for real. Maybe not a pennant, but surely a solid finish in the first division. They spun the turnstiles even more merrily. On August 11 the Pirates won their fifth straight, Bob Friend beating Warren Spahn, 6–4, for his 15th win, though Face had to come in for the last out, and in the stands on that Monday night were 38,932 fans, second largest night crowd in Forbes Field history. Clemente had two hits.

The next day George Witt, who never gave up a run anymore, spun a two-hitter as the Pirates massacred Milwaukee, 10–0. Actually, it was closer than that, a 2–0 game until the eighth, when Pittsburgh exploded for eight runs as 36,867 looked on. Clemente had one hit and stole a base. The club passed San Francisco, and trailed Milwaukee by five. The next day the string was seven wins as Clemente went wild, with home runs in the first and second innings, and four runs batted in in a 10–9 win over Philadelphia. The winning streak was the longest in nine years.

The Pirates were not going to catch Milwaukee, this season. Nobody was. As the Pirates won, so did Milwaukee. And Pittsburgh still remained streaky, suddenly dropping four games out of its next five. In the game the club won, on August 16, Frank Thomas had his greatest day of the year, with three home runs and six rbi in a 13–4 win over Cincinnati. Bob Friend won his 16th, and stood 16-and-12.

On August 20 the Pirates were again third, with a 62-and-56 record, but again the team got hot. Red hot. Bob Clemente had sagged to .275 after he'd played 113 games, but now he'd rip the ball at a .340 clip the rest of the way. And with Friend, Witt, and Raydon virtually unbeatable, the shakedown was over, the true cruise underway.

Clemente had four hits on August 23. The next day, Friend became the first pitcher in the league to win 17. Three days later the club won its 67th game, the most wins by any Pittsburgh team in nine years. They won that one big, 14–1, over St. Louis, with 18 hits. Clemente had a single and a double, and he stole another base. Two days later Friend won number 18, beating the Braves, 3–2, and the team trailed by 6½.

On September 1, in a doubleheader split with Philadelphia, Forbes Field attendance went over one million, the first time since 1950. The next day indefatigable Bob

Friend won his 19th, as Clemente had a single and a triple. George Witt, who had won six straight games, sat on the bench these days because his right elbow was inflamed. But on September 5 he returned to shut out Milwaukee, 1–0. Bill Virdon ripped a home run in the tenth inning. Clemente went 2-for-5.

The next day, pinch hitter Johnny Powers came off the bench to hit a home run in the eighth and beat Milwaukee, 7–6, and Pittsburgh again passed the Giants.

Curt Raydon whipped Milwaukee, 11–1, on September 8, moving his mark to 8-and-4, but the big news was Clemente. No man in baseball history has ever hit more than three triples in a single ball game. A few men have hit three, including Willie Mays. On September 8, Clemente hit a triple in the fourth inning, again in the fifth, and a record-tying third triple in the eighth. The young line-shot hitter had moved into the record book.

The next day Pittsburgh whipped San Francisco twice, 4–3 and 2–1. In overtime the next day Clemente singled with two out in the tenth inning, at Forbes Field, and big Stuart whacked a mighty home run off Marv Grissom, to beat the Giants again, 6–4.

This was Bob Friend's 20th win, the first Pirate 20-game winner since Murry Dickson, in 1951. But Friend was not finished. He won his 21st on September 14, edging Chicago, 5–4, as Clemente began a modest hitting streak of his own. On September 16, Pittsburgh beat Chicago twice, 2–1 and 3–1, and the 2–1 game was Red Witt's seventh straight. Witt now led the league in earned-run average.

Bob Friend won his 22nd three days later (and his sixth straight), the most wins by any Pirate hurler in three decades. Pittsburgh kept winning (though so did Milwaukee), and on September 20 the club stood at a lofty 84-and-65. In the preceding month, Pittsburgh had won 22 games and lost nine. But they would not win another. The next day Milwaukee clinched the 1958 pennant, and Pittsburgh suffered a natural letdown. When it ended, Pittsburgh solidly held second place, four games ahead of San Francisco. And the team had its heroes. Friend, with 22-and-14, had his greatest season. Dick Stuart, coming up on July 10, hit 16 home runs, at least one in each park, and Forbes Field had a new slugging idol. Two slugging idols. Frank Thomas belted 35 home runs, and 109 rbi. Bob Skinner batted a robust .321, with 13 home runs and 70 runs batted in. Dick Groat posted a .300 mark. Bill Mazeroski hit 19 home runs, most ever by a Pirate second baseman. Bob Clemente, coming off his .253 season in which he played just 111 games, now socked a solid .289. His ten triples were among the league's leaders. He knocked in 50 runs; he stole eight bases, and—best of all—he played in 140 games, sore arm, sore back and all. And the two kids, Witt and Raydon, had won 17 games, Witt nine and Raydon eight. No wonder the fans gurgled at what lay ahead.

8

"Purkey Was the Worst"

IF THE BEAUTY of baseball is epitomized by two unknown rookies storming the big leagues and winning 17 games while losing just six, then the tragedy of baseball is not far removed. Toss the same coin, and it comes up tails, or it falls through a grate. With arms like buggy whips, rookies George Witt and Curt Raydon had fogged baseballs past the league's greatest hitters. Had he pitched more innings, George Witt would have been the official earned-run leader in 1958. Curt Raydon was not far behind.

Where are they today? Who knows? They won 17 games in 1958. In 1959 they won no games at all. Pain and inflammation suddenly gripped Red Witt's right elbow. The arm that hurled baseballs through cement now could not throw baseballs through paste. And Curt Raydon, whose talent had burst full in 1958, suddenly could not get a man out. Four days after the season had started, Raydon was optioned to Columbus in the American Association. He never rejoined the Pirates. Witt lasted longer, to lose eight ball games and win none in 1959, throwing at half speed and without the crackling curve of a year ago.

So they come up, and so they go down. It is the cruelty of baseball, its inexorable way. Karl Spooner pitched two shutouts in his first two starts in the National League, in 1954. Soon his great left arm became sore, and soon he was finished. Herb Score, the Cleveland southpaw, seemed headed for the same sort of immortality that belongs to another Cleveland fireballer, Bob Feller. But a line drive hit straight back by Yankee Gil McDougald struck Score in the eye, and he never was the same. Bill Delancey, Cardinal catcher of the Gas House days, fell victim to tuberculosis at the very start of his career, and was dead on his thirty-fifth birthday.

But not all the drama is that of men who appear today and disappear tomorrow. Bob Friend had been around Forbes Field since 1951. Seven very long and difficult years later, he won 22 games in a single season, most by any pitcher in his league. The next year, 1959, he would lose 19 games, most by any pitcher in his league. Baseball has its mysteries, enigmatic, insoluble.

The Pirates who had finished so strongly in 1958—84 wins, second place—suddenly had to make up the loss of 17 games won by Witt and Raydon, and the difference between Bob Friend's 22 wins in 1958 and 8 wins in 1959.

They made up some of them, but not all, and in 1959 the club finished fourth.

And Bob Clemente? A seesaw pattern seemed to have been established, bullish in the even years, bearish in the odd. Clemente had hit a fair .255 in his freshman season of 1955. The next year he zoomed to a crackling .311. Then he plummeted on that teeter-totter in 1957 to .253, missing over 40 games with his lame back. Again he rebounded, in an even year, playing 140 games, hitting a solid .289.

In 1959 the Pirates lost Witt's and Raydon's arms, and Friend's winning skills. The year also saw Bob Clemente play fewer games in a single season than he had ever played in the big leagues. On May 25 the Pirates placed Clemente on the disabled list. He did not return to action until July 5. He got into 105 games, some of these merely in running or pinch-hitting appearances.

The right arm, hurt by a sidearm throw early in 1958, began to plague Clemente early in 1959. An errant pitch in a game had struck his elbow, aggravating the injury. He could not throw, and a Clemente without his throwing gun is a sheriff with his bullets removed. Nor could he freely swing his bat. His arm, as he had put it, hung to the ground.

Part of the problem was worsened by the earliest start in baseball's history. The teams went at each other beginning on April 9. Snow still covered much of the country. But even without the chilly start, Pirate fans could read a bleak forecast ahead. On April 4, brash first baseman Dick Stuart missed a team bus to Tampa, during the spring training, and Danny Murtaugh fined him $100. (The next day Stuart homered in a 5–1 win over Philadelphia.) George Witt had to leave the box in the first inning of his last pre-season outing because his elbow hurt him.

But not all was bleak. Pittsburgh had come so close in 1958. As 1959 opened, the team seemed much stronger. In a move hinted ever since Frank Thomas had his run-in with Bobby Bragan in 1957, the slugger was traded during the baseball winter meeting to Cincinnati, for third baseman Don Hoak, catcher Smokey Burgess, and pitcher Harvey Haddix, and at three positions the Pirates had suddenly bolstered themselves. If not at bat, surely in the field, and in 1959 Thomas was to hit 70 points less than either Hoak or Burgess. Haddix would win 12 games.

So the season began brightly enough, except for the weather. Maybe the weather would warm up, and Red Witt's arm would come around. He was young and strong. In 1958 the elbow had fired up occasionally, but always the pain had subsided.

On April 9, in Cincinnati, Ron Kline faced ex-Pirate Bob Purkey, and Pittsburgh was beaten, 4–1. It marked the fourth time without a loss Purkey had beaten his former mates. Bob Clemente went 1-for-4 that opening day, which sounds like little to rave about, except when Clemente got a hit off Purkey it really was news. In a six-year stretch, Clemente would collect exactly ten hits off Purkey. His average in that period hovered at or below his weight, .176. Later, Clemente would look over the roster of National League pitchers and he would say:

"Lots of pitchers give me trouble. Drysdale, Marichal, Jim Maloney . . . But Purkey was the worst. He threw lots of bad balls. I hit pitches I like, no matter where they are. But I couldn't hit Purkey's bad pitches."

So a hit off Purkey wasn't bad, and it knocked in the Pirates' lone run. The next day, Warren Spahn blanked Pittsburgh, 8–0, but Clemente had two hits, and the following day Lew Burdette edged Vernon Law, 4–3, as Clemente again had two hits. It snowed the next day, and a fretting Danny Murtaugh confirmed what was apparent. Curt Raydon, mysteriously, had lost his stuff. Raydon went to Columbus, his major league career abruptly ended. Bob Purkey came back against Pittsburgh and beat them again, 3–2, and then Red Witt went a painful six innings, losing to Cincinnati, 10–5. Pittsburgh had not won a game.

They didn't win the next day, but they didn't lose, rain stopping play after nine innings, and a 2–2 tie with the Braves. Clemente got the tying run with a home run in the top of the eighth, off Bob Rush.

The tie was a good omen. Vernon Law, not pitching very well, still outlasted Milwaukee on April 18, 11–5, to post Pittsburgh's first win and Milwaukee's first loss.

But it was a cold year. Literally. Cold weather forced postponements; so did rain; and cold and rain are not what the doctor orders for sore arms. Clemente's arm ached unwaveringly. When the Pirates could play again, finally, they whipped Cincinnati with an astounding comeback, seven runs in the seventh and two more in the ninth. On April 25, behind Harvey Haddix, the Pirates won again, 4–2, the game marked by one of those electrifying moments that make baseball so exciting a sport. It is the unexpected that thrills us—the catch of the uncatchable drive, the seven-run rally, the clutch hit by a so-so hitter. This time Bob Clemente was on first base, Virdon on second, and Smokey Burgess at the plate. Burgess ripped a base hit to right field, where Cincinnati's Wally Post—young and strong, and with a powerful arm—scooped up the ball and readied himself to make a play. But there was no play, because the speedy Virdon was nearly home, and the speedy Clemente was moving to third, so Post did what so many outfielders will do. He nonchalantly lobbed the ball toward second, to make sure Burgess ventured no farther. And Clemente kept right on running, to score from first on a single. His arm hurt, yes, but not his whippet legs.

Four days later, trailing 2–0 in the seventh, Pittsburgh rallied for three runs and a 3–2 win. Clemente opened that seventh inning with a triple.

But we are picking our days. In between, the Pirates

floundered, and Clemente with them. He had a three-hit day on May 2, but before the game he was hitting .246. He wasn't saying much, but you could tell by looking at him. The arm bothered Clemente. The pain was intense, and it threw his entire game out of kilter. He did not hit; he did not field; he could not throw. He made an error on May 11; he made two errors in a game the next day against San Francisco. Not that he was the only Pirate in difficulty. Bob Skinner ran into a fence and hurt his back, returned, and went into a horrendous slump, 0-for-30. ElRoy Face, who could not lose a game—he hadn't lost since May 30, 1958, and would not lose until September 11, 1959—nearly lost his hand. He broke a water tumbler in a St. Louis hotel room, and needed five stitches to piece two fingers together.

On May 17, in a doubleheader split with Chicago, Clemente seemed well again, or surely well enough. He belted a home run in each contest, but a pitch caught him on the right elbow, and he had to leave a game in St. Louis two days later. He did not return until July 5. On May 25 he went on the official disabled list, which meant he was off the playing roster forty days. The team had been playing well enough the past two weeks, and when Clemente left, the Pirates stood 20-and-18, in third place. The next day, May 26, 1959, the Pirates lost a ball game that can rip the heart out of a club.

Harvey Haddix pitched twelve perfect innings that night—a no-hit ball game, without a single base runner—yet managed to lose. He pitched it on a muggy night in Milwaukee, which means he faced the better hitters in his league, Joe Adcock, Hank Aaron, and Ed Mathews—but better or not, they all were helpless, thirty-six of them, for 12 innings. Lew Burdette also had his stuff that night—not perfect but good enough—and though Pittsburgh rapped 12 hits, not a Pirate scored. Haddix's 12 innings went for naught. Still, they stand as the greatest 12 innings a major league hurler ever threw, and they deserve passing mention. Of the 36 batters who came up and went down, empty, in those 12 innings, Haddix—whom they called Kitten—was behind just twice. Haddix had everything, but mainly he had unerring control, and a great slider. Twice he struck out big Joe Adcock with the slider, but the third time was the charm—the unlucky charm. In the thirteenth, the slider betrayed him. Actually, it was his defense that first betrayed him. Felix Mantilla opened the bottom of the thirteenth with a ground ball to Don Hoak. Twelve men before Mantilla had hit the ball into the dirt that night, and twelve times Pirate infielders had thrown them out. This was the thirteenth, and it came in the thirteenth inning. Perhaps that is what did Haddix in, too many thirteens. Don Hoak fumbled the grounder, then threw it low. Rocky Nelson, at first, might have salvaged the out had he come up with the low throw. It skipped off his glove, and Mantilla became the first Brave runner, on Hoak's error. Eddie Mathews sacrificed, and up stepped Hank Aaron, hitting .442. Haddix purposely walked Aaron, and then tried another slider to Joe Adcock. This one came in high, and Adcock lofted a fly ball that just cleared the fence in right-center field, and Pittsburgh had lost, Haddix had lost, and if a single game in May can make or break a team, this game broke Pittsburgh.

Bad luck pursued Pittsburgh from then on. Two days later, Joe Christopher, subbing for Clemente, dove for a drive and cut a deep gash in his left hand, winding up in the hospital. Early in June, base runner Smokey Burgess put his head in front of a thrown ball; nine days later Bill Mazeroski saw his string of 216 games broken when he sat on the bench with a sore left leg. On July 10 the Pirates lost two catchers in one game. Burgess split a finger behind the plate, and Hank Foiles tore his left knee. Later, third baseman Hoak would be spiked by the Giants' Daryl Spencer, and Red Witt never got over his disabled elbow.

Bob Clemente chafed on the bench. But the rest did him good; it may, indeed, have been the most important 40 days of his career. For when it ended, Bob Clemente never again would sit out so many ball games, never again find himself so physically useless. In a later year, he would suffer from malaria, but even then—sick and weak as a cat—he played a game here, a game there, and when the season had ended, he'd missed just ten ball games, and he'd been well enough in the other 152 to lead the league in batting.

He was inserted into the game of July 5 in a late inning, and the Pirates won a doubleheader that day. It marked the team's 81st game, though Clemente had played but 34. From that moment, he missed just two contests.

He played his first full game since May 17 on July 9, as Pittsburgh beat the Cubs, 4–3. Somehow he had not lost his batting eye (or you might say he had gained it back again); he was 2-for-4 that day. Face won his 13th straight, without a loss. Yes, the Pirates had lost 17 wins from Raydon and Witt, and another 14 when Bob Friend dipped from 22 wins to eight. But little Face made up a bagful all by himself. And nearly all by himself he had Pittsburgh up in the first division, with a 44-39 record, just three and a half games behind leading San Francisco. Sparked by Face, and by the return of Clemente, Pittsburgh won seven of eight games early in July. Clemente was not tearing the league apart, but his average started to rise. By July 18 he was hitting .263, but from then on out, he did tear the league apart.

On July 18—batting leadoff—he had three hits and a stolen base. Four days later, he had three more hits. Two days later, his batting average was up to .281, an increase of 18 points in six days. He had three hits on July 28, and two the next day, and by July 31 it was .290. The rest of the team had stopped hitting—in one stretch of nine games the club scored just 13 runs—so they needed every hit. They got every hit on August 6 as the Pirates massacred the Cardinals, 18–2, with an outburst of ten runs in the ninth inning. Clemente had a "meager" 2-for-5 that day; the rest of the club had 21 other hits. A few days later, the Pirates beat the Cubs, 4–3 in 14 innings, as Clemente had three hits and scored the winning run. It marked Pittsburgh's 14th overtime win against one loss—Haddix's "perfecto."

On August 12, Clemente did most of the damage in beating Philadelphia's Robin Roberts. An early-inning double got the Pirates one run, and a bases-loaded triple in the seventh broke a 2–2 tie. Two days later Pittsburgh edged Milwaukee, 2–1, as Clemente scored one run and knocked in the other.

Three days later, Clemente celebrated his twenty-fifth birthday, but Clemente never has had a field day on his birthday. Not that he would have grabbed Pittsburgh headlines. For on August 18, 1959, Branch Rickey—fifty-two years older than Clemente—resigned as chairman of the Pirates to head up the embryonic, soon aborted, Continental League.

It had no effect on Clemente's hot bat. He had moved up to .304 after his 74th playing date, was horse-collared in three trips the next day, and then in a double win over

Los Angeles, Roberto had five hits. ElRoy Face won one of those two games, and Face's record was now 16–0. The club had a day off, and spent it losing an exhibition with their farm team, Columbus. Red Witt lasted less than one inning.

On August 28 Vernon Law beat Philadelphia, 9–0, for his 15th victory against seven losses. Clemente had an inside-the-park home run, his fourth and last homer of the season, and now his mark was .307, eleventh best in the league. But his bat cooled, and though Pittsburgh played well—as well as any team in the league, the fans responding in increasing numbers—the pressure of ill luck and ill health kept Pittsburgh from mounting a serious charge. Not that the league needed a fourth contender. This was the year the Dodgers, Braves, and Giants waged their furious struggle, with the Dodgers finally sweeping the Giants four straight up in Seals Stadium, and then edging the Braves in a two-game play-off. Still, Pittsburgh did finish a strong fourth, five games back of San Francisco, and part of that strong finish was Clemente's own finish. He had cooled off early in September, but again he started to hang out frozen ropes, five hits in a double-header at Chicago, three hits a few days later, two hits the next day, and a final average of .296. No, it wasn't a good year in Pittsburgh, the solid club rated no worse than 5–1 to win the 1959 pennant, the club with a peck of power and all those strong young hurlers; and no, it wasn't a good year for Clemente, despite his .296 average, seven points up over the year before. You can't count it a good year when you sit out 47 games, and when you wonder whether you will ever play a full season up to your potential. Would the years slide by as they had in the past, years that marked him a good player, *but*—a good player, *but* he was far too injury prone, a good player, *but* he knocked in too few runs, a good player, *but*?

The last year of the 1950s had passed into the record books. Now it was a new decade. The decade of the sixties. The decade of Bob Clemente. No buts.

9

"Beat 'em, Bucs!"

FOR ALL the years in the cellar, all the years of frustration and defeat, the Pirates and pennants form a parlay that goes back to the dawn of the century. In 1900, Barney Dreyfuss selected Fred Clarke, a twenty-four-year-old center fielder, to manage his Pirates, and the Pirates finished a strong second. The following season Clarke led the club to Pittsburgh's first pennant. Power, speed, and effective pitching marked the 1901 Pirates. Shortstop Honus Wagner batted a lofty .351, while stealing 48 bases. Manager Clarke hit .316, and stole 22 times. Ginger Beaumont hit .328, with 32 steals. First baseman Bill (Kitty) Bransfield posted a .292 average, and stole 28 bases. Jack Chesbro led all National League pitchers, with a 21–9 record.

The next year, the Pirates improved. Spitballing Chesbro won 28 games, and in 1902 Pittsburgh took the pennant by one of the greatest margins in league history. Pittsburgh won 103 games and lost just 36, for a .741 percentage, beating the runner-up Brooklyns by 27 games! The .741 winning mark has been bested just once in the majors since, by the 1906 Cubs, with 116 wins and 36 losses.

In 1903 the Pirates won again, whipping McGraw's Giants by six and a half games. Again pitching turned the trick, the club reeling off 15 straight wins in May and June, highlighted by six consecutive shutouts. It didn't hurt that Wagner led the league in hitting, with .355, ripping 30 doubles and 19 triples among his 182 hits. The hulking shortstop with hands the size of scoop shovels would lead the league eight times in twelve seasons, and some veteran baseball men consider Wagner the finest player that ever lived.

Still, none will contend that the Pirates, through the century, have dominated the league. They won pennants in 1901–1903, and in 1909, and again in 1925 and 1927, but until 1960, that was all. Over three decades had crawled by since the last pennant flag, and even that last pennant reminded all of the ignominy of the 1927 World Series crushing by Babe Ruth and his Yankees.

In 1960, a cry sprang up in old Forbes Field, a ball park built in 1909, a pennant year, and named for General John Forbes. Forbes had defeated the French at Duquesne in the French and Indian Wars, and promptly renamed the city Fort Pitt. Forbes did not do this all by himself. Battles, like pennants, are team tasks. Forbes had a pretty fair regimental commander, a colonel named Washington who later went on to some fame, winning the 1924 World Series.

The cry that sounded through old Forbes Field was—"Beat 'em, Bucs!"

It was a cry that gathered strength in the middle innings of a ball game—almost any game—and swelled to a thunderclap as the game inched into the ninth. Teams that win pennants must win the tight games. At Pittsburgh, in 1960, the wins couldn't have come any tighter. The Pirates won 21 games in 1960 in their last at bat. Twelve times they won after two men were out in the last inning.

They beat 'em, did the Bucs, in 1960, but seldom was it easy, seldom was it a series of laughters, those games you roll up six- or seven-run leads, and laugh all the way home. The Pirates laughed, all right, but only in the clubhouse, and the sound had a high edge, nearly hysterical. They beat 'em, these Bucs, but they did it like a man climbing a cliff by his fingers. Only when you got over the top and lay flat on the safe ground, gasping for breath, could you sigh your relief . . . if you had the strength. Such was 1960.

It began on April 12, in Milwaukee, and the result was a one-run margin, but not for Pittsburgh. Joe Adcock hit a two-run home run in the eighth inning off ElRoy Face, and the Braves won, 4–3. It was a hard game to lose, almost impossible, in fact. Batting in order, Dick Groat, Bob Clemente, Bob Skinner, and Dick Stuart had eight hits among them. When you pack eight hits in a bunch, you have to score runs. But Pittsburgh didn't, and the Pirates moved back to Forbes Field for the home opener, wondering whether they would repeat 1959, when the club lost its first five games.

In that home debut, the Pirates put together all those hits again, and this time logic prevailed. The hitters scored runs, and when the cannonading was over, it was a laugher after all, 13–0 over Cincinnati. Clemente had three hits in three licks that day, two doubles and a single, plus a sacrifice fly, and after two games Roberto was hitting .714, and leading the league. Behind him came the Pirates' captain, Dick Groat, at .625. Clemente also led with six runs batted in, and for the first time he would really drive in base runners all season, 94 rbi in 1960.

Two days later, on Easter Sunday, the Pirates won two games from Cincinnati, 5–0 and 6–5. In the first, Clemente had a home run and a triple. But Pittsburgh lost as many as it won the first week, and on April 19 it stood 3–3. Then it began to jell.

"To win, you must play as a family," Clemente said later. "In 1960 we were a family." And Clemente, for a spell, was Papa.

Vernon Law won his second game on April 20, edging the Phils, 4–2. The next day Clemente—batting cleanup—had three hits, and the Phils had again been whipped, 11–5. The Pirates won nine straight, longest Pittsburgh streak in 15 years. On April 22, Clemente rifled a line-drive home run off Milwaukee's young Joey Jay with a runner on, to help beat the Braves, 6–2. Two days later the Pirates moved into first place, licking Milwaukee, 7–3, as Clemente had three hits and scored two runs. This was Vernon Law's third straight. Bob Friend then shut out the Phils, for his third in a row, striking out 11 batters. By April 29 Clemente was hitting a mammoth .396. And there were laughers. On April 30 the Pirates scored ten runs in the second inning to win, 12–7, over Cincinnati. Bill Mazeroski, who had looked like a fine hitter in 1958 but then had turned up fat in 1959, was his lean self in 1960. He had a field day on that last day of April, with a single, two doubles, and a home run, and merrily into May laughed the Pirates. They won another on May 1, as Clemente hit a grand-slam home run off Don Newcombe in the first inning, Pittsburgh slaughtering Cincinnati, 13–2, as Law won his fourth.

They didn't win every game. Face, who had won practically every game in 1959—18-and-1—now lost his second game of 1960, but Pittsburgh picked right up again. Clemente had a single, triple, and home run on May 5, the home run his fifth of the young season, and Pittsburgh spoiled Lou Boudreau's managerial debut with the Cubs, 9–7. Clemente now had 22 rbi, to McCovey's 21. Clemente got another the next day in Candlestick Park, an incredible 450-foot home run blasted into the teeth of a crosswind off Sam Jones, but Clemente did little celebrating. Jones gave up just two other hits as San Francisco beat the Pirates, 5–1, and in the ninth inning, after he had popped up, Clemente threw his helmet in disgust, and umpire Shag Crawford ordered Roberto from the field.

You don't win pennants by 27 games anymore. At least not in 1960. The Pirate lead faded and disappeared as the club hit a sour note, in the field. The next day the Giants came from behind with six runs in the seventh inning to win, 6–5, but mainly it was porous defense that did the damage. And on May 8 the Giants completed a three-game sweep, 13–1, before 40,173 delighted Bay fans, as Pittsburgh committed seven errors, three by Dick Groat. San Francisco led Pittsburgh by two games.

Shakily, the Pirates moved down the Coast to Los Angeles, and lost again, 7–4, as winless ElRoy Face was beaten the third time. But you could not blame the pitching. The Pirates made four errors (Clemente one of them), for 15 errors in the last five games.

Yet when the year was over, what marked the team was the few mistakes the Pirates actually made. The team snapped back, with a more typical performance the next day. On May 11 the Pirates scored five runs in the last two innings, to beat Koufax and Los Angeles, 6–3. Clemente was 2-for-5 against the great Sandy, and Face—at last—won his first game of 1960.

The grim pennant struggle was on for earnest. For two months and two weeks, the Pirates would edge to the top and slip back again, as the Giants and then the Braves took turns sliding past Pittsburgh, with St. Louis always close by. The ability to come from far back marked the Pirates; no matter how badly they played on a given day, you never knew for sure they wouldn't explode in the last inning or two to recoup it all. On May 13 Pittsburgh left its bats home for six innings, trailing Milwaukee, 2–0. Then the bats appeared, for eight runs in the seventh inning. Dick Groat had six hits—three doubles and three singles—moving his average from .277 to .318. The next day the two clubs fought ten dogged innings, tied 4–4, and in the eleventh, with two out and two on, Clemente laced a triple off the left-field fence, inches above Wes Covington's leaping glove, for a 6–4 win. Clemente hit safely in 12 straight games, and on May 18, Pittsburgh and San Francisco had again tied for the lead, each with a 20-and-10 mark. The next day Pittsburgh beat the Cards, 8–3, with 13 hits, as the Giants were rained out. Clemente chipped in two doubles and two singles.

Then the Giants came to Forbes Field, and it was Revenge Days. Yet they did not come easy. On May 20, the Giants scored a run in the twelfth inning to go ahead, 4–3, but in the bottom of the twelfth, Don Hoak singled, Groat doubled him home, and with two out, Clemente singled to right to win the ball game, 5–4, while 39,439 fans—second largest night crowd in local history—roared, "Beat 'em, Bucs!"

It was the team's fourth straight, and ninth win in the last ten games, but San Francisco did not lie down. The Giants beat Bob Friend, 3–1, the next day, and this time the crowd was the largest Saturday afternoon throng in Forbes Field history. Sunday's was a dogged, murky affair, rain twice delaying the game for a total of 63 minutes, and again it went extra innings. Clemente opened the bottom of the eleventh with his third hit, a double, and after two men were walked, catcher Hal Smith singled Clemente home, for an 8–7 win and a game and a half lead over the hated Giants.

But you don't win all the tight ones. Sandy Koufax came along to very nearly do what nobody has yet done: pitch a no-hitter in Forbes Field. Sandy's was a one-hitter, beating Bennie Daniels, 1–0, on May 23. The Dodgers won again the next day and the next, and suddenly Pittsburgh wasn't first anymore. But on May 27 the Pirates made a deal that strengthened the club where it needed it most. Pittsburgh bought left-handed Wilmer (Vinegar Bend) Mizell from St. Louis in return for Julian Javier, a brilliant Columbus farmhand who was obviously destined for greatness at second base. Pittsburgh had all the greatness it needed at second base, and it could use a southpaw starter. Pittsburgh immediately began to win again. On May 28, Clemente got caught in a rundown between third and home, but he barged into Philadelphia catcher Jim Coker, who dropped the ball, and Pittsburgh had the tying run in a 2–2 game. Then Hoak banged a two-run home run in the thirteenth.

The club tied for the lead on May 29, and two days later played another cliffhanger. With the score 3–3 in the eleventh, two men walked, Dick Groat bunted for a base hit, and Clemente singled off young Jay Hook, to beat the Reds, 4–3. The month of May ended with Pittsburgh out in front, by a game and a half over the Giants. Clemente was hitting a solid .353, to lead the league by four points over Joe Adcock, and a few days later Roberto was voted player of the month in the National League. He'd hit .336 in May, with 25 runs batted in in 27 games.

When the year had ended, only Clemente, of all the Pirates, could point to a batting average that not for a single day had dipped below .300. In later years when bitterness seemed to mark Clemente's memory of the 1960 season, remember that unwavering average. Other men had great seasons: Dick Groat, superb in the field, sharp at bat, and an inspirational leader at all times; Dick Stuart, with the long ball; Don Hoak, raw spirit on the field, plus timely hitting and the best defense at third base since Pie Traynor. Law would win his 20, Friend 18, and ElRoy Face would save two dozen games and post a 2.90 e.r.a. in 68 appearances, most in the league. But Clemente knocked in more runs that did big Stuart, more than Hoak or Skinner, and nearly twice as many as Dick Groat. Clemente fielded his position like a magician, catching and throwing as well as any man in the league. Nobody threw out as many men as did Clemente, with 19 assists.

"It was my best year," he would say a few years later, even after he had led the league in hitting two years in a row, and three times in five seasons.

They named him player of the month in May, but to some he remained player of the season. Early in June, the Giants had the first three pitchers in earned-run averages, young Mike McCormick, Billy O'Dell, and Sam Jones—but the Pirates had Clemente's big bat, and they led the league. In June the Pirates threatened to put away all opposition. Law became the first pitcher to win ten games, Pittsburgh grabbed a four-game lead, and the jittery Giants fired manager Bill Rigney and hired Tom Sheehan. By the end of June, Clemente was hitting .333, but teammate Groat now stood at .334. Clemente, of course, was the big rbi man, with 52. Groat would not knock in 52 runs all year.

But you cannot make final judgments on such matters.

Who knows who is the most valuable player? Spirit enters into the argument. Groat, everyone has said—and it is true—inspired his teammates. Groat drew out of them their finest potential. Groat was, and is, brainy; he will someday manage a ball team, and he will manage it superbly well. So how do you assess these things? Yet Clemente had qualities that did not show themselves only in the final statistics. He too had spirit, a fiery quality that burned with a dark light. He did not urge on his teammates by words; he did it by example.

On July 1, in Los Angeles, the Pirates got into yet another dogfight, dragged into extra innings. With two out and speedy Joe Christopher on second base, Clemente stepped in to face Johnny Podres. Podres quickly whipped over two strikes, and Clemente, upset with himself, went to the dugout to change bats. With his new weapon, he did not exactly overpower the next pitch. He chopped a bounder over the box behind second, where Pee Wee Reese collared it, but Clemente had himself an infield hit, and Christopher, running with two out, slid home safely. Then Dick Stuart dropped a pop single in front of huge Frank Howard in right field, and Clemente ran right though a stop sign at third to score all the way from first. The Pirates needed both runs. Los Angeles scored a single run in its last lick, and Pittsburgh had won another squeaker, 3–2. In the clubhouse Clemente said happily, "My foot was sore. I ran all the way home so I could rest it on the bench."

Clemente slumped briefly in early July and sat out a few games. On July 10 the Pirates whipped Gene Mauch's Phils, 6–2, and when the game was over, Mauch said what others were thinking: "The more I see of them, the more I like the Pirates."

The Pirates? Win a pennant? The unthinkable was

thought, and now said aloud. The crowd urged, "Beat 'em Bucs!" and they beat them. Clemente had three hits that day, and Pittsburgh led Milwaukee by five. But nobody counted their chickens. Two weeks later, to the day, Milwaukee won a doubleheader and the Pirates lost one game to San Francisco, and the Braves took over the league lead, with a 52-and-36 mark, to Pittsburgh's 53-and-37. The difference was two percentage points.

To some it appeared that the bubble had burst. The unthinkable was unthinkable, after all. Now you would see the Pirates collapse. Wasn't this the pattern? The early charge, the late fade?

On July 25 Pittsburgh beat St. Louis, as Virdon, Skinner, and Clemente hit home runs. Clemente had a second hit, and Bob Friend won his eleventh. Milwaukee was idle, and Pittsburgh edged ahead by half a game.

The Pirates never again were second. Team pitching now matched team hitting. On July 29 Mizell pitched a two-hit shutout. Six days later, Red Witt—who had not won a game since 1958—went six strong innings against Los Angeles, yielding five hits and one run, and Pittsburgh beat the Dodgers, 4–1. (Witt never won again in the majors.) The next day Mizell pitched another shutout, beating San Francisco, 1–0. He had help. In the seventh, a Giant batter ripped a line drive toward the fence in right field. Clemente raced for the ball and, at the last moment, dove headfirst toward the concrete. He caught the ball with one hand, and then smashed with sickening force against the wall. He fell to his knees, got up groggily, blood spurting from his split chin, but the ball was held. They rushed Clemente to the hospital; he took five stitches and sat out five games, but the second day he was back, August 13, he put on a field day. The Pirates beat St. Louis, 4–1, as Clemente knocked in every run. He, too, had help. Groat went 4-for-4. In the first, Groat tripled, and Clemente singled him home. In the third, Groat doubled, and Clemente hammered a home run off Ray Sadecki. In the fourth, Virdon walked, Groat singled, and with two out Clemente singled home the fourth run, and Pittsburgh had won 13 of its last 18 games.

The next day Vernon Law won his 17th, and a few days later Clemente had four hits in seven times at bat in a double win over Philadelphia. He did more than hit. In the eighth inning of the nightcap, with the score 3–3, the Pirates suddenly bunted Robin Roberts out of his serene old mind. Groat, Skinner, and Rocky Nelson all bunted for base hits, and Clemente stepped in. Unnerved, Roberts fired four pitches outside the strike zone, and a newly matured Clemente let them pass by, for a run-scoring base on balls.

Now the Pirates were red-hot. A home stand in August ended with a 14-and-4 record. On August 24 the Pirates exploded with 17 hits against Chicago. Clemente had four, including his tenth home run. Never had he hit more than seven home runs in a single season. In 1960 he would belt 16, and begin a string of years of double figures in home runs. The hot streak ended with four straight losses, three of them to the Cards, but the cold spell was temporary, and the Pirates rolled on, beating 'em all. On the 29th, Clemente had two hits as Law won his 19th, whipping Los Angeles, 10–2. The next day Groat and Clemente hit home runs, to knock out Koufax in the fifth inning and beat Los Angeles, 5–2. And on the last day of August, Clemente belted his twelfth home run, with Groat on, to set back the Giants in San Francisco, 7–4. Groat led his teammate, .323 to .319, but Clemente was supplying the big bat, the big hits. He kept supplying them. On September 1 his three-run home run helped lick San Francisco,

6–1, and three days later his fourteenth home run helped nip the Phils, 5–3, as the Pirates stretched to a six and a half game lead. So when Dick Groat stepped in front of a Lew Burdette pitch two days later and fractured a bone in his left wrist, it did not seriously matter. You cannot lose a man like Groat and not suffer, but this was not a one-man team, and the lead—swollen to seven games—held up. On the day Groat broke his wrist, Clemente had two doubles and a single, and the Braves were beaten, 5–3.

It ended on Sunday, September 25, not with a win, but with a Cardinal loss. All the others had been put out of reach, and now it would be the Cards, shut out by Chicago's Glen Hobbie. When news reached the Pirates in Milwaukee, Bob Clemente was getting ready to bat. He heard the commotion on the bench, and he turned to the next batter, Dick Stuart, and asked, "We win it?" Then the public-address announcer confirmed that the Pirates had indeed won it, and Clemente joyously ripped a base-hit to center, off Warren Spahn. When Hal Smith doubled, Clemente ran through another signal at third, to score in a belly-whopping cloud of dust.

"Stop at third?" he said later, incredulous. "I want to get to the bench quick, and talk about winning the pennant."

That was the pennant. More lay ahead. The Yankees. Mickey Mantle. Roger Maris. Whitey Ford. Elston Howard. The big, bad, great Yankees. Thirty-three years earlier, these same teams had met in a World Series, and Pittsburgh did not win a game. A myth has grown out of that Series to the effect that the Pirates of 1927 quit before the first pitch, just from watching the Yankees take batting practice, Ruth, Gehrig, and the rest smashing ball after ball out of sight. Pie Traynor, of that '27 Pirate team, hoots at the charge. "We never saw the Yanks take batting practice," Traynor says. "We were in the dressing room at the time, for a team meeting."

No matter. Myth or not, the Yankees won four straight, and Pittsburgh writhed for 33 years in disgrace. Babe Ruth had belted two home runs and knocked in seven runs; little Mark Koenig had outhit the Babe by an incredible 100 points.

But this wasn't 1927. Every year is a new war. And the Pirates knew about wars.

They even looked war-weary. Clemente did not feel well. He had burned himself out during the race, and now he felt tired, sore, worn dry. His mates were no better, even worse. Law had sprained a tendon in his right ankle on September 26. Groat's broken wrist had mended, just. Skinner had a jammed thumb.

Something else—not physical—was bothering Clemente. As always, baseball writers assessed the players of each team before the first Series game.

"When the papers describe all the Pirates," Clemente said later, "you know what they say about me? 'Good fielder and good runner.' That was supposed to be my contribution. What about my hitting and the runs I batted in?"

He'd hit .314, fourth best in the league, behind Groat (at .325), Norm Larker, and Mays. He'd knocked in 94 runs, best on his club.

So all was not smooth, all not family-ish, as Roberto Clemente went into the Series. He is a proud man, and his pride had been hurt. Already it was being said, aloud and in print, that teammate Groat was a shoo-in for the league's Most Valuable Player award. In Clemente's heart, he felt he—not Groat—deserved the award. This too ruffled the smooth waters, made it less a family and more a collection of individuals, with individual traits, individual vanities.

Into the Series he went, tired, disturbed, hurt. Yet no other man on either club hit safely every game. True, he did not hit with power, but he hit steadily, every day. Nine hits in seven days, for a .310 average. (Groat, his wrist obviously sore and his batting eye rusted, batted .214 and committed two errors.)

In the first inning of the first game, the Yankees scored a run, but the Pirates scored three times. Virdon walked and stole second, Groat doubled, Skinner singled and stole second, and Clemente singled. Clemente's hit knocked Art Ditmar out of the box. The first inning edge held up, just, Pittsburgh winning, 6–4.

Then the deluge. Mickey Mantle pounded two home runs the second day, and a third the next day, while Bobby Richardson hit a bases-loaded home run on his way to a record-setting 12 rbi for a single Series. The Yankees won, 16–3 in Pittsburgh, and 10–0 in Yankee Stadium.

In New York, standing outside the Commodore Hotel where the Pirates bedded down, Clemente heard a passerby jeer at the Pirates. Bill Surface, in his excellent book, *The World Champion Pittsburgh Pirates*, tells of Clemente's reaction, prophetic and earnest.

"When we no have good pitching," Clemente replied to the passerby, "we look like minor league team. But tomorrow Law is pitching and Face is ready in the bullpen. We win. You come back tomorrow."

Law went six and a third innings, giving up two runs, and Face went the remaining two and two-third innings, giving up nothing (though helped mightily by a great catch by Bill Virdon), and Pittsburgh won, 3–2. This was the Series—the Pirates won the tough ones, the Yankees won the laughers. After the 3–2 win, the Pirates jolted the Yankees again, 5–2, and the two clubs returned to

Pittsburgh for the sixth and seventh contests. The Yankees resumed their bludgeoning, crushing Bob Friend and his relief, 12–0. In their three wins, the Yankees had outscored Pittsburgh, 38 to 3. In their three wins, Pittsburgh had outscored New York, 14 to 8.

So it came down to the seventh game, on October 13, before 36,683 fans, and what a game they saw! In the first two frames, Pittsburgh scored four times. With Law pitching, it seemed more than enough. But Law faded in the fifth, and Face replaced him an inning later. ElRoy did not have it. With two men on, Yogi Berra hit a just-fair home run to put the Yankees ahead, 5–4. In the eighth, the Yanks scored twice more, off Face, and when Pittsburgh came to bat, the score was 7–4, and though the fans yelled, "Beat 'em, Bucs!" it was more prayer than expectation.

They beat 'em, anyway. Gino Cimoli popped a single into right center. Bill Virdon hit a double-play grounder toward Tony Kubek, but the ball took a freakish hop and jammed Kubek in the Adam's apple. Kubek, hurt and speechless, came out, and clutch-hitting Dick Groat singled sharply to left, scoring Cimoli, leaving the Bucs behind by two. Skinner bunted the runners up, for the first out, but Rocky Nelson popped out. Now it was up to Clemente. Jim Coates had replaced little Bobby Shantz. Clemente tapped a high bounder past the mound, down to Bill Skowron, the first baseman. But neither Coates nor Bobby Richardson covered first, and Clemente outraced Skowron to the bag for a single. One run scored, and the Pirates trailed by one. Catcher Hal Smith blasted a tremendous drive over the left-field wall, and suddenly Pittsburgh led, 9–7. But the Yankees did not quit. Bob Friend pitched, and little Bobby Richardson singled. Pinch-hitter Dale Long (remember Dale, and those home runs, as a Pirate?) also singled, and Harvey Haddix replaced Friend. After one out, Mickey Mantle singled for one run, Long taking third. Then Yogi Berra ripped a ground ball down the first-base line, where Nelson made a superb backhanded stab. Nelson elected to retire Berra at first, which automatically removed the force play on Mantle. Mickey shrewdly dove back for the bag, beating Nelson's desperate return dive as Dale Long romped home with the tying run. Skowron grounded out, and into the bottom of the ninth it went.

It went two pitches. Big Ralph Terry had picked up for Jim Coates, and Terry missed with his first pitch and got his second over the plate, but fat. Bill Mazeroski shot it out over the left-field wall, for a home run and all the marbles. Or at least $8,417.94, if you didn't want marbles. Forbes Field went wild; Pittsburgh went wild. Mayor Joseph Barr—according to Bill Surface's book—leaped to his feet and threw out his arms, nearly knocking his wife, Alice, cold. Then Mayor Barr went into the Pirate clubhouse where Dick Stuart doused him with a can of beer. Manager Murtaugh was in a state of delirium. His wife later said, "I never saw you so happy, Danny," and the jut-jawed Irishman replied, "If you had been standing on one side of me, and Bill Mazeroski on the other side, and somebody said I had to kiss one or the other, it wouldn't have been you."

Hysteria. But not all happy. Into a bar in Torreon, Mexico, walked glum Antonio Duenas, a house painter. "The Yankees gave the Series to the Pirates," said Duenas. Bartender Gaspar Sanchez—a Pirate fan—shot him dead.

But that was far away, unknown. The Pirates got ready for a big victory celebration in Webster Hall Hotel. Bob Clemente did not stay around for it. He flew home, instead, to Puerto Rico. For years it has been said, "Clemente turned his back on his teammates."

Clemente is not a partying man. The clubhouse had been party enough. When you search for pictures of that last game, you come across a photo of Hal Smith crossing home plate after his dramatic three-run home run. Clemente is grabbing Smith, and with just his hands on Smith's upper arms, he has lifted the big backstop off the ground, in joy, in delight, for Smith, for himself, for the team.

Clemente did not turn his back on Pittsburgh, even if he did turn down the victory party. He wandered out of Forbes Field that late afternoon, and the streets were full of people, laughing, happy. Never had Clemente felt so close to the people of the city. The moment was like a Mardi Gras, a festival, not unlike similar holidays on the streets of San Juan. He walked with the people, mingled, just another human being in the universe of humanity, caught up in the sea of joy, of oneness.

"I felt like one of them," he said, simply.

Then he went home.

10

Batting King: 1

CLEMENTE WAS HOME when the selection of the Most Valuable Player was announced: Dick Groat, Pirate shortstop and captain and the league's leading hitter in 1960. Few people were surprised.

Still, Clemente had hoped he might win. So he searched the list for his name. Second, perhaps? Third? At least someplace in the top three, the top five. Clemente ended up eighth. Teammate Don Hoak, a fiery competitor, a great glove man, a good clutch hitter, wound up second. After Hoak came Willie Mays, Ernie Banks, Lindy McDaniel, Ken Boyer, Vernon Law, and then Clemente.

Clemente could not easily swallow the vote. Three teammates—Groat, Hoak, and Law—had been deemed more valuable. He became bitter. The bitterness lasted; it coated him, cloaked his relations with the press, even with his teammates. Nor does he deny it. Four years later, on his thirtieth birthday, he said, "I was very bitter. I still am bitter. I carried the club all year. I was the only batter to hit over .300 all year. Never under." He said more. Groat, he acknowledged, had a fine year, but "he was out a month." (Groat played in 138 games to Clemente's 144; Groat came to bat 573 times to Clemente's 570.) Nor was it a case of underestimating his fellow players. "Sure the other players were great," he said. "But I was great, too." Not that he deemed the award more important than the team victory. "I'm a team player," he said. "Winning the pennant and the world championship were more important to me than my average. But I feel I should get the credit I deserve." Part of it lay in his treatment by the press not only before the World Series, when Clemente felt he had been dismissed too lightly, but during the Series as well. "I had a hit in every game," Clemente said, "but the only way you could find my name in the paper was with a magnifying glass."

There is this about many Latin ballplayers. They are absolutely honest. They say what they mean; they mean what they say. If something bugs them, they let it out in the open. They do not sulk; they do not quietly let a hostility fester. They invariably speak it. And they care deeply, for all the alleged whistling in the clubhouses. They have never learned the Stateside way, the cynical way, the so-what way. If it matters, it matters, and it cannot be buried or so-whatted away. In a sense, they are the innocents of baseball. They believe, often, in absolute truths, in goods and bads. They avoid the middle ground of gray. Ask a Latin ballplayer how he feels and he will say, "Very good," or "Very bad." Ask the Stateside player the same question, and he will answer, "Pretty good," or "Not so bad." The Latin player often speaks of goods and bads. They are, invariably, a deeply religious, deeply moral group of people. They have not really learned, as the Americans in the States have learned, to compromise with moral absolutes. Perhaps it is immature of them. The world is not that clear-cut, not that divided into goods and bads. The world of *maybe* is huge, almost total. But the Latin eschews it with a fierce devotion to truth in the extreme.

Roberto Clemente has many names on the Pirates. His mates call him Robby, Bob, Roberto. His mother calls him Momen. Vernon Law—and this is ludicrous—calls him Herschel. Quietly, behind his back, they have called him Goldbrick and Crybaby and the like. But beginning in 1961, they started to call him, good-naturedly, "No Votes." Mark the name, and mark the open use of it. It may mark the change that had to begin sometime in Bob Clemente, and help him recognize the world of maybe, of good-and-bad combined, of gray. The failure to win the acclaim he felt he deserved had eaten a hole in Roberto Clemente. His teammates knew how he felt, but they also thought it was funny. They ribbed him. Nor can it be said they were and are wrong, and he right, or the other way. It did bother him that he had not won, and it does embitter him still, or it did until the vote of 1966. And it is funny.

So "No Votes" came into being. But even before, and more importantly, another name took hold in Forbes Field. It began to sound through the old stadium about the time the fans started to chant, "Beat 'em, Bucs!" When Roberto Clemente came to the plate or made a startling play in the field, fans chanted, "*Arriba! Arriba!*"

Pirate broadcaster Bob Prince helped start the *Arriba* bit, or at least goaded it on. *Arriba* seems to have many meanings. I am not versed in Spanish slang, so I must go to my dictionary for help. It means "Up there," I am told, which has some relevancy, such as suggesting Clemente hit a pitch out of the park, "up there" in the seats. It also seems to mean "Hurray!" which is better, or "Let's go!" which is best. But whatever it means, it took hold, the fans going ape over their new idol.

If a handful of newsmen were going to ignore Clemente's contribution to his team in an annual vote, at least the fans recognized his worth.

So bitterness ate a hole, but a fandom's warmth and appreciation quickly plugged most of it.

Besides, spring comes once a year, and when it does—down in the Florida camps—it is warm and full, and a winter's ache begins to melt away. The sun shone at Fort Myers, as newsmen clustered about the now World Champion Pittsburgh Pirates. The title itself tasted good. The team nobody expected to win a pennant—ever—the lowly Pirates, beaten and beatable, were now World Champions. They had humbled the mighty Yankees.

Newsmen clustered about Groat and Hoak and Law and Face and Danny Murtaugh, but they also surrounded Roberto Clemente. They asked him how he felt, a polite first question to most players, but to Clemente it touches an essential part of his being. He answered fully. "I had a very bad winter," he told a man from *Sports Illustrated*. "I eat the wrong food or too much food or not enough food. I don't know. Now I feel good, real good. I still watch my diet. No fries. I am healthy. This year I play much better."

He checked in at a strong 180-plus pounds. He knew the summer would melt away a lot of that weight, perhaps a dozen pounds, so he wanted to start in as heavy as possible. Heavy, within Clemente's lean frame, that is. You cannot picture Clemente fat. He had played just one month of winter ball. He felt strong, ready. George Sisler, batting coach, eyed young Clemente. He took him aside and he said, among other things, Clemente could win the batting title in 1961. Clemente—it has since been reported—registered surprise at Sisler's remark, though Roberto had come close enough the year before. Surely the idea had to have entered his head. He knew he could hit. It was something he had always known and had proved to everyone's satisfaction all through 1960. Perhaps his surprise was that if he'd taken it for granted he might win a batting title, why hadn't Sisler as well?

Nor would the bitterness inside Clemente deter him. It would provoke him to greater effort. If the newsmen refused to acknowledge his value in a year he batted .314 and led his team in rbi, perhaps he could persuade them in a year he batted still higher. Bitterness is not the key to Clemente. It marks him as an honest man, yes, but it must be put in its place, and its place is secondary. He is a team man, he wants to hit because if he hits, the team scores and wins, and this is what counts in baseball. And, of course, he is a proud man, who must prove himself and remove for all time those qualifying words of praise—a good player, *but*. No buts.

A few years ago he had picked up a light bat, in the mode of other players. But now he was his own man. He knew his strengths and his flaws, and he adapted his bat to them. In 1961 he switched bats again, going for a heavier model, up from the 32–33-ounce bat to one of 36 ounces, and an inch longer than his old 35-inch weapon. The problem was not whiplashing home runs out of sight. Not in Forbes Field. He would slow up his swing, control it better, improve his timing and make sure he made contact. The home runs would fall in, as they always did for good hitters. Meanwhile, he would satisfy himself with hits, more hits, and still more hits. Hits like a stream of bullets from an automatic gun. Hits sprayed to all parts of all fields. This was the secret of his success, and he knew it. Let the wild gunners swing their toothpicks. He would aim his bludgeon.

Not that he didn't want home runs. Every man does. Dick Stuart announced in 1961 how much he admired Clemente and his batting prowess. Clemente looked over at big Stu and replied, "I'll tell you. I would love to have his power. I could make $200,000 a season with his power—and my brains."

Stuart swallowed down spoonfuls of honey before a game, to give him strength. So Clemente took to doing the same. He went into 1961 with a heavier bat, a stronger back, and desire goaded both by bitterness and by a fan's welcome.

This would be the year of the hitter, the year Roger Maris and Mickey Mantle made their twin assault on Babe Ruth's mark of 60 home runs, and Maris would erase the mark. It would be the year an unknown freshman hitter named Norm Cash would slug the ball at a .361 clip, and more men would hit more home runs than ever before. In the American League, two teams had been added to the roster, the Los Angeles Angels and the Washington Senators (as the old Senators moved to Minnesota). With two teams made up principally of has-been and never-was pitchers, the hitters feasted. But even in the National League, hits would crash like sustained thunder. Orlando Cepeda would batter 46 home runs, and Willie Mays 40. Frank Robinson would rip the league apart, with 37 home runs and 124 runs batted in. Young Vada Pinson would hit a rollicking .343.

It was a year of more than baseball. John F. Kennedy took office in a swirling snow; Yuri Gagarin orbited the earth; the Bay of Pigs stained American history with shame. Patrice Lumumba was murdered in the Congo; Dag Hammarskjöld died in a plane crash trying to effect a cease-fire in that dark infant nation where Lumumba's murderers became heads of state. The world throbbed with the passions and tensions of sporadic wars.

The day before Yuri Gagarin stepped into his spaceship, the Pirates began their title defense, and it seemed like 1960 all over again. With two men out in the ninth inning, and two men on, and Mike McCormick, the 1960 e.r.a. leader, on the mound for San Francisco, Bill Virdon crashed a home run, to win the season opener, 8–7.

But it would not be 1960. The one-run games would be lost this year. The next day, Bob Clemente dropped a foul fly hit by Giant rookie catcher Tom Haller. Haller then homered to tie the game at 1–1. In the eighth inning the usually unerring Vernon Law hit Orlando Cepeda with the bases loaded, and the Giants led, 2–1. In the ninth the Pirates rallied, but Bob Clemente grounded out with two on and two out, and the Pirates had lost.

Still, there was no sign of disaster. The Pirates soon stood 5-and-3, Dick Groat had an eight-game hitting streak, and Clemente started a ten-game string, broken, naturally, by Bob Purkey. Roberto was hitting a big .360, and on April 29 Pittsburgh beat Cincinnati, 6–3, to take over the league lead.

But the eye of the fan kept turning away from Pittsburgh. Warren Spahn pitched his second no-hit, no-run game, this time against the Giants, winning 1–0. Two days later, one of the men he victimized, Willie Mays, hit four home runs in a single game, and the first month had ended. Clemente was hitting .323, but who could notice when Wally Moon was batting .417?

He made you notice. On May 6, in Pittsburgh, Clemente had a triple and three singles, in a perfect 4-for-4 day, and now his average was .367. The next day, courageous Red Witt retired the first 16 batters, but then his arm gave out, and Los Angeles and Koufax beat Pittsburgh, 4–2. Clemente had two hits. Two days later, he drove in four runs on three hits, including a home run off young knuckleballer Eddie Fisher, and the average had soared to .391. He was shut out the next day, and in anger at plate umpire Frank Secory's strike call in the ninth inning, he threw his bat, and Secory threw him out. Though the name Clemente means mild, gentle, Clemente has never pretended to be a meek-mannered man. *Arriba*, with its r's rolling like thunder, is more like it.

Now it was Cincinnati's turn to streak, taking nine straight before Pittsburgh beat the Reds on May 12, 8–5. The Pirates beat 'em again the next day, and moved back on top. On May 24, Clemente blasted two home runs to help whip the Cubs, 7–3, but all was not well. A few nights earlier Murtaugh had decided to bench Stuart and use Rocky Nelson in a game against Milwaukee. Miffed, Stuart disappeared from the dugout before the game. Murtaugh traced him to the clubhouse where Stuart was sealing a letter he'd just written his wife.

"The stamp will cost you $50," Murtaugh snapped.

Murtaugh did not know that Gino Cimoli was also in the clubhouse. He'd been shining his shoes when Murtaugh barged in. Hastily, Cimoli hid in the men's room.

Perhaps it was overconfidence, perhaps the edge of losing hones a man, and the satisfaction of winning blunts a man. On two occasions Don Hoak ate out Stuart for what Hoak considered a lack of hustle on the bases. "If you can't give us 90 feet," Hoak once snarled, "why don't you stay in bed?"

The family was bickering. Stuart and Bob Friend came close to blows one day when the pitcher accused Stuart of pursuing a ground ball too leisurely.

The team did not fall apart. Yet. San Francisco led the

early going, with 22–13, followed by the Pirates, a game behind, and the Dodgers and Reds, within two games of Pittsburgh.

But they kept limping, not running. Literally. Red Witt—who probably symbolized the 1961 club—was struck on the right ankle by a line smash off the bat of Cardinal outfielder Don Taussig. In falling, Witt managed to sprain his left ankle. One pitch, two ankles. On June 5, Vernon Law pitched a strong seven innings against Los Angeles to win, 5–2, but Law's right shoulder pained him, and he had to leave. Law's record was 2-and-4 at the time; he would win just one more game all season. On July 7 he went on the disabled list, and was through for the year.

Clemente had his minor difficulties. They are the kind that come with fame. Dick Ellsworth brushed Clemente on May 30, and Don Hoak, in anger at the Cub hurler, had to be restrained by an umpire. Two days later it was Lew Burdette's turn to knock Clemente down, and Burdette was ejected. This was the testing period. The word had gone out: Knock Clemente down; he becomes too angry to hit. Clemente agrees. "I used to let brushback pitches bother me. I used to get so mad I tried to get right up and hit a home run on the next pitch. Rocky Nelson talked to me. He said they always do that to the most dangerous hitter. Now I get up and stay calm. I get up and hit line drives. They don't knock me down so often."

Another Clemente trait. He took the brushback pitch as an act of dislike, not a baseball stratagem. And Clemente, perhaps more so than most, likes to be liked.

They had reason to like him, the fans. His skills kept refining. This would be the year his batting reached a personal high, yet he did not neglect his fielding. On May 13 Cincinnati catcher Bob Schmidt looped a fly ball to short right field. Base runner Gordon Coleman, on first, headed for second. But when Clemente ran in, hands up as if to catch the fly, Coleman retreated to first. Then the ball dropped in front of Clemente (who knew all the time he could not reach it), and Roberto picked it up and fired to second, for a force play on Coleman. George Sisler said it about his batting, but it pertained to his total game. "Clemente's got good common sense. He uses his intelligence along with his ability."

His bat, warm in May, heated up as summer approached. He had four hits on June 14, and scored two runs, as Pittsburgh shaded Cincinnati, 5–4. He had two hits the next day, but then Bob Gibson blanked him, and the next day Clemente did not play. His stomach was upset; it is another of those chronically tender parts of Clemente's anatomy. He returned with two hits, and then missed another game, and then came back just in time for a painful defeat that stigmatized the team. On June 23 the Pirates methodically battered Philadelphia for five innings, building up a 9–0 lead. The Phils scored a couple, but so did the Pirates, and going into the eighth, it remained 11–2. A laugher. Lock it up and take it home. No sweat. The Pirates sweated. The Phils scored four times in the eighth and six in the ninth, to post a stunning 12–11 win. The Pirates made four errors, for four unearned runs. It was not the mark of a champion. Clemente had three hits, for a .332 average, third best in the league. Teammate Don Hoak led, at .342, but nobody was whistling; the team stood at 32-and-38, in fourth place, seven games back of Cincinnati.

The next day, Clemente hit two home runs. Three days later he had four singles, and on June 30 he was named the starting right fielder on the National League All Star team. Only Frank Bolling, at second base, polled more votes than Clemente. At the time of his selection, Clemente was batting .338, with Chicago's George Altman leading at .347 and Hoak next at .344. But before the game, Clemente would change that considerably.

On July 6, in a doubleheader in Chicago—where Clemente hits better than in any other park in the league—Roberto had five hits in five at bats in the opener. He scored four runs and drove in five, as Pittsburgh massacred the Cubs, 15–3. In the second contest—won by Chicago, 5–1—Clemente had two more hits. Altman did not have a bad day, going 4-for-7, and the lanky outfielder now led Clemente, .356 to .351.

Clemente went hitless the next day, but he had another perfect game on July 8, 4-for-4, in a 4–3 win over Milwaukee, and he had shaved Altman's lead to two points. The next day, Clemente went ahead. He had two more hits, as Altman was going 1-for-8 in a doubleheader, and at the All Star break, Clemente was hitting .357 to Altman's .349. They never caught him.

The hot bat continued right into the cold winds of San Francisco, where the All Star game was played. He crashed a mighty triple to right-center field off Whitey Ford, and scored when Bill White drove out a sacrifice fly. Later with Willie Mays on third, Clemente hit a sacrifice fly. Then, in the tenth inning, with the score tied and Mays now on second, Clemente ripped a Hoyt Wilhelm knuckleball into right field for a game-winning single.

It remains one of the big moments of Clemente's career. He said after the game, "When I get the big hit in the tenth inning, I feel better than good. But what makes me feel most good is that Danny Murtaugh let me play the whole game. He pay me big compliment. I think I do not let him down, no?"

Roberto Clemente. The man who likes to be liked. Today he wears not his 1960 World Series ring, but his 1961 All Star ring.

But the All Star game is just a trinket. It is the pennant games that count. The team remained in San Francisco, and Clemente had two hits on July 13; the next day he hit the team's first grand-slam home run of the year; two days later he had three more hits, including another home run. The team wallowed in the second division, dropping five in a row and seven of its last nine in July, but Clemente kept ripping. He had his fifteenth home run on July 22, and his sixteenth—to tie his previous major league high—on July 29. He had two singles and a double the next day, and then came the second All Star game, this time in Boston, where the wind didn't blow; it just rained. Clemente was hitless in two trips. He admitted he was tired. The season had been long and dreary for Pittsburgh, after the title run of the prior season and the high hopes for this season. "I'm dead tired already," he said, as the players headed for Boston. "Last year, when we were winning, I wanted to go to the park every day. Now I'm dragging myself."

But he was not ready for the tomb. On August 2 he had just one hit, but it was his seventeenth home run, and the next day he had an incredible day against St. Louis. The Pirates all had incredible days, shelling the Cards, 19–0, with 24 hits. Clemente had five straight hits, each coming after two strikes. He was hitting .366 after the contest, but the next day Bob Purkey, his nemesis, blanked him. Sometimes when a man is blanked after a torrid hitting binge, he remains blanked for a spell, cooling out. Clemente had two singles and a triple the next day, and in a Sunday doubleheader on August 6, he went 5-for-9, socking a home run and a double in the first game, and three singles in the second. Now he was hitting .371. He had one hit the next day, and then he did cool out, hitless in a double bill in Philadelphia. But in the week before, Clemente had 20 hits in 36 times at bat, for a .556 mark; he had eight extra-base hits and 33 total bases.

He could not keep up the .371 average. But he never really slumped the rest of the way. That week in August had clinched his first batting crown. Nor was it a Punch-and-Judy performance, full of leg hits, bunts, and Texas leaguers. Clemente hit his nineteenth home run on August 10, and his twentieth the next day, off Robin Roberts. His 73 runs batted in, of that date, stood sixth best in the league. He had three more rbi the next day, and a home run the next. Warren Spahn broke an eight-game streak, but the next day Roberto blasted a home run off young Don Cardwell who the year before had pitched a no-hit game. Clemente ended August at .360. In the field his throwing terrorized the league's swiftest runners, yet he still threw out more men—many more—than any outfielder in baseball. Sometimes he did more than collect an out. On August 8 his throw to the plate nipped the Phils' Tony Gonzalez, and when catcher Hal Smith tagged Gonzalez a bit energetically (and right on the mouth), Gonzalez got up swinging. In no time, seven separate brawls broke out on the diamond. Manager Gene Mauch wound up with a black eye; Danny Murtaugh received a spike wound in the neck. By the time the season had ended, Clemente had an unbelievable 27 assists and had partaken in five double plays. Nobody in the 1960s has thrown out as many men in a single season.

But he still did not get the attention all this deserved. Maris and Mantle had stolen the headlines. In his own league, people searched for more colorful stories. Giant manager Al Dark became angered over a Giant defeat in

Philadelphia, threw a stool across the clubhouse, and a piece of a finger with it. Later Dark cornered his pitchers in another tense clubhouse and told them they were gutless quitters. Ancient Warren Spahn won over 20 games, again. Other men lost games; the Phils lost 23 in a row. All this attracted more notice than did Clemente, the league's new batting titlist. The rancor within took on added taste. In 1961 a young man from the Virgin Islands, Alvin McBean, joined the Pirates. McBean is a highly intelligent, highly articulate human being. He roomed one season with Clemente and got to know the outfielder better than did most men. Clemente, said McBean, was his idol, and ought to be other people's idol. But he did not get the publicity a man that good ought to get.

"He thinks the press doesn't like him," McBean said later. "I think they don't like him either. The paper should read, 'Bob Clemente and the Pittsburgh Pirates will be in town tonight . . .' That's how the story should begin. Clemente first."

McBean studied his friend and teammate, and this is how he saw him:

"Robby loves his image. He takes good care of it. He is wary of being with people he does not approve of. He believes people know you by the company you keep, so he keeps careful company."

How about the injuries, the upset stomachs, the complaints?

"Robby likes to talk about how he feels. He complains a lot. He wants you to talk to him, make him feel good. When he says he feels terrible, I tell him he feels good, that he can really hit the pitcher going against us, that he'll go 4-for-4. He will say he has diarrhea or he feels weak. I tell him he is fine. He has his own routine for keeping up his strength. On the road, he gets up late for breakfast, takes maybe a 30-minute walk, and then he goes back to bed. He used to say to me, 'The more you rest, the prettier you become.' He is set in his ways. He does not like noise. But he is a great player. If he were on the Yankees, Mickey Mantle would be nowhere. That's how good he is."

All this is one man's opinion, a quick sketch of another man, a look at his insides, the way his mind and psyche work.

But—as we have said—Clemente is a ballplayer, and that is how we must eventually judge him. On September 3, he blasted his twenty-third home run, this man often written off as "a good hitter, but no power." He hit no more home runs that year, tired and wan, the club mired in sixth place and the fans no longer chanting, "Beat 'em Bucs!" The fans chanted nothing. They stayed home. On September 23 the Pirates lost the year's longest game, a 16-inning contest, to last-place Philadelphia. Clemente ended the season on a negative note. He was struck on the right elbow by Don Drysdale, and forced to sit out the last five games. Attention riveted on the Cincinnati Reds as they headed for their first pennant in over 20 years. The Pirates helped them out. On September 26 Pittsburgh's Joe Gibbon shut out Los Angeles on one hit, to eliminate the Dodgers and clinch it for the Reds. It also ended Pittsburgh's one-year reign as the league champion.

But it began for Roberto Clemente his years of supremacy. He had hit .351, to whip Vada Pinson by eight points. Clemente had 201 hits, most for a Pirate since Paul Waner. They were big hits—30 doubles, ten triples, 23 homers. In his 146 games, he batted in 89 runs; he scored an even hundred. Stan Musial eyed the final figures, and he said of Roberto Clemente: "He is a fine, all-around player, good defensively, and good at bat, and getting better all the time."

Not exactly lyrical praise. Not quite what a batting king usually hears.

So the decade was two years old; Clemente had hit .314 and .351. Clemente had knocked in 183 runs and scored 189. He'd finished just shy of the top one year and far ahead of his league the next. But the praise was tepid. Some things do not change.

11

"Mama's Boy . . . Goldbrick!"

THE LATIN AMERICAN baseball player lives two lives. One, in the States; the other, at home—Puerto Rico, the Dominican Republic, Venezuela, Panama, wherever. In one life, he is treated as a curiosity, a stranger, an outsider. In the other, as a human being, and sometimes a national hero.

After the 1961 season and his first batting title, Clemente went home. In the States he had received some praise, but not much. Joe L. Brown shrewdly assessed Clemente as "the best right fielder in the business, a ballplayer who has never been fully appreciated."

But in Puerto Rico the story was different. People stopped and stared at Clemente in the streets of San Juan. Kids clustered about him. When he sat in the Red Rooster restaurant, on the corner near the ball park of the San Juan Senators, a few doors from the Caribe Hilton, more children stood outside and pressed noses against the restaurant window, just to watch their idol.

Magazine writer Howard Cohn journeyed to Puerto

Rico in the winter following the 1961 season, and spoke with Clemente. In his own environment, Clemente becomes a more expansive person, more willing to speak out. He is, after all, more comfortable at home. He spoke to Cohn—and later the words appeared in *Sport* magazine—about the growth of interest in baseball in Latin America, and the implications of the growth.

"Kids in Puerto Rico played the game because it was fun," Clemente told Cohn. "We never were as determined about it as even the smallest boys seem to be in the States. Very few of us ever thought about pro ball in America, and I was no exception. Besides, American baseball seemed so far away. With all the talent there, why should teams be interested in players on the Island?"

But then came Bobby Avila and Minnie Minoso, and all this changed.

"The success of so many Latins recently seems to have made everybody American-baseball conscious. Kids here are getting more and more like your kids, following U.S. box scores, rattling off statistics, and all hoping some day to be major leaguers, too."

But success—in the States—posed problems, and Clemente touched on them. Cohn wrote:

"Latin American Negro ballplayers are treated today much like all Negroes were treated in baseball in the early days of the broken color barrier. They are subjected to prejudices and stamped with generalizations. Because they speak Spanish among themselves, they are set off as a minority within a minority, and they bear the brunt of the sport's remaining racial prejudices. They have been stripped in many baseball minds of individual identities. Some players and managers lump together the Latin American Negroes with a set of generalized charges as old as racial-religious prejudice itself. 'They're all lazy, looking for the easy way, the shortcut,' is one charge. 'They have no guts,' is another. There are more."

Cohn asked if it was because he was Puerto Rican and not born in the States that Clemente received less publicity.

"What else can you think?" Clemente replied.

At another time, in another place, Clemente expounded further on the problem:

"Latin Americans need time to get adjusted. We lead different lives in the United States. We're always meeting new people, seeing new faces. Everything is strange. The language barrier is great at first. We have trouble ordering food in restaurants. You have no idea how segregation held some of us back. We Latins are people of high emotions, and coming to this country we need time to settle down emotionally. Once we're relaxed and have no problems, we can play baseball well. The people who never run into these problems don't have any idea at all what kind of ordeal it is."

The Latin Negro lives in the worst of all possible worlds when he plays ball in the States. He is Latin, which means the average American conceives of him as a man from a hovel, or from a tree, a man who carried water on his shoulders and cut sugarcane and is good for little else. He is a school dropout, a man with a sullen face and a grudge against the world, a man who has come to the States seeking the pot of gold, the rainbow, or at least an easy drunk to roll.

And he is Negro, with all the clichés that attach to Negroes: lazy, uncaring, criminal, dirty.

Men are more complicated than that, whether black or white or yellow, whether Puerto Rican, American, or Chinese. There are dirty whites, and sober blacks and God-fearing Mongols. There are brave men of all hue, and honorable men and dedicated men. They come in all shapes and colors and from all parts of the world. Felipe Alou carries a New Testament in his back pocket at all times. Clemente honors his mother above all people in the world. Orlando Cepeda plays baseball on a knee twisted beyond belief.

So when Clemente—or anybody—reveals himself as a man with a low threshold of pain or a man with occasional jealousies or petty angers, remember the rest. He is a man, with the strengths and frailties of the species.

One frailty, after the 1961 season, lay in his elbow. He went to a hospital to have a bone chip removed—a surgeon had located it under X ray—but when he was under the knife, they could find nothing. The elbow had healed itself. Perhaps he was a hypochondriac, after all.

Later, he played ball in San Juan, and when he showed up at Fort Myers, prior to the 1962 season, he appeared not quite the robust man who had trained there a year ago and then went on to win the batting title. He weighed in at 172 pounds, ten below his 1961 figure. Part of the reason for the loss of weight, Clemente said, lay in his stomach. It was often upset, and when it wasn't upset, it just plain hurt. Doctors diagnosed it as a nervous stomach, which does not make it hurt a jot less.

He took the nervous stomach into 1962. At first, it didn't matter. On April 10, in the season opener, he hit a bases-loaded home run against Philadelphia, to help whip the Phils, 6–0. The team, hoping to make amends for the dismal sixth-place showing and 75-and-79 record of 1961, won its first ten games, and the field rocked again with "Beat 'em, Bucs!" But it was too streaky a club, not solid at all, and after the winning streak it dropped nine out of ten. Nor did Clemente keep up that first day's work. He had three hits in a win over the Mets on April 14, and a home run two days later to help beat Chicago, and a week later another three-hit day against the Mets, but then the multiple-hit days came farther apart. Perhaps it was his strength, or lack of. Those ground balls he used to shoot through the open spaces of the infield were now gobbled up and hurried into double plays. By the season's end, Clemente had grounded into 18 double plays, which put him up there with the leaden-footed leaders.

By May 26 he was hitting .256, this man who usually starts as though he'd taken batting practice a month longer than anyone else. He became somewhat disgusted with himself. Later, he looked back and said, "I sure wasn't hitting with power, like before. Not so many extra-base hits. I swung hard, but the ball didn't jump off the bat and go very far."

Sound awful? Like a guy about to hit .256 all season?

Clemente ended at .312, eighth highest in the league. His .256 average had sprouted. On May 30 he had two singles and a triple against the Cards; two days later it was a single, double, and homer against the Colts, and the next day a three-run home run to beat the Colts. He hit his second grand slam of the season, to whip Milwaukee, 9–7, and when the All Star game rolled around, he was again the starting right fielder. Why not? He was now hitting .336. Nor did he stop. He upped it to .347 by July 21, but that was his high. Perhaps his low weight did work against him. Now the season sun baked him even more lean; his weight plummeted to 162 not nearly enough for a man to take to the plate against the hard-throwing pitchers of the National League, Koufax and Drysdale, Juan Marichal and Bob Gibson, and all the rest, men who can knock a bat out of a man's hand as easy as popping stovepipe hats off with a well-aimed snowball.

He sagged in August and September, and when the

year had ended, so had his brief reign as the league's batting king. Now there was a new king, Tommy Davis, of the Dodgers.

Still, how bad a year was it? A solid .312, which left his career average at an even .300. He also now had five career grand slams, which left him behind Willie Mays by just one and Mickey Mantle by two. His nine triples were among the league leaders. He had collected 19 assists. It would have been more, except the league had learned not to run on Clemente's arm. He walked 35 times, not much for a good hitter, but many more than those early years when Clemente swung at anything in sight and a few pitches not yet visible. Opposing pitchers walked him nine times intentionally.

You can't make more of it than it was. His power had fallen off. Ten home runs in 1962, as against 23 the year before. Seventy-four runs batted in, down 15 from the year before.

Nor could you make it less than it was. Eighth best in the league, ahead of such hitters as Cepeda, Mays, and Ken Boyer. "I felt weak most of the season," Clemente said, and one wonders how weak he has to feel before he really stops hitting.

The Pirates made a fine comeback in 1962, except again you hardly noticed. This was the year of Sandy Koufax and his sore index fingertip, the ensuing collapse of the Dodgers, the charge of the Giants, and the spine-tingling three-game play-off to determine the pennant winner. Pittsburgh ended a strong fourth, with a 93-and-68 record. Teams have won pennants with 93 wins. This, also, was the year of expansion in the National League—the New York Mets and the Houston Colts made it a ten-team league—and attention focused on these new teams.

So you saw the frenzy at the top of the league, the Giants and the Dodgers, and you saw the foolishness at the bottom, in New York and Houston, but you didn't see the middle ground where Pittsburgh lay. Dick Groat had another fine year, at .294 (*funny how one man has a fine year at .294 and another man a disappointing year at .312)*; young Donn Clendenon got into 80 games and belted .302; Skinner also hit .302. Bob Friend won 18 games; Vernon Law, battling that sore shoulder, was 10-and-7. But other men fell down. Big Dick Stuart, object of furious booing by Pittsburgh fans, slumped to a feeble .228. Bill Virdon hit just .247. Joe Gibbon hurt his arm in spring training and went on to a 3-and-4 season.

Attendance fell, too, to a total of 1,090,648.

And it all got worse, for Pittsburgh, before it got better. Much, much worse.

Roberto Clemente had played his one thousandth major league ball game in 1962. His own shakedown cruise was long ended. Neither George Sisler nor his manager nor anyone was likely to make much impression on Clemente's style or his potency. He had become, for want of a better word, established. He said, after 1962, "I will come back next year. And this time I will hit good."

Yet how much better was he going to hit? Lifetime average of .300, going into 1963. A man who would surely hit, but again you heard those *buts*. No power, they said. Never had knocked in a hundred runs, they said. Except for one year (which must have been a fluke), seldom hit many home runs.

All true to a degree. And to a degree, he did come back in 1963, and hit good, or well, or whatever adverb described Clemente. He batted a solid .320, second best in the league, as Tommy Davis hit .326 to win back-to-back batting crowns. With his .320 mark, Clemente outhit Hank Aaron by a point and Willie Mays by six.

He hit 17 home runs, again a solid figure, up from ten of the year before. He had eight triples, again with the league's best, and triples have always marked the combination of speed and power. It also marks the exciting ballplayer. No moment in baseball is more exciting than the line drive belted to the farthest fence, the race around the bases as an outfielder runs down the ball and heaves it to a cutoff man who then fires on a low line to the third baseman.

So it was a good year, base hits and power, and excitement, and even 12 stolen bases. You knew from the steals that Clemente had to feel better; surely his back did not bother him. Very little bothered him, physically. For the first time he played over 150 games—152—and it would begin a string of such years.

Yet in such a healthy year, he had his worst run-in with a manager, and it stemmed from Clemente's history of aches and ills.

There were earlier moments that season when Clemente had his miseries, but they were not physical. In a ball game against Chicago, he stepped up against right-handed Glen Hobbie, the bases loaded, and hit a torrid line drive down the first-base line. The Cubs' Merritt Ranew, usually a catcher but on this day playing an unfamiliar first base, stabbed the drive, stepped on first, and fired to second—and Roberto Clemente had hit into a triple play.

On May 16, in Los Angeles, in a game the Pirates would lose, 1–0, Clemente bunted and roared down to first. The Dodger second baseman Jim Gilliam hurried over to cover first, and as Clemente's foot touched the base, the throw to Gilliam was still two feet short of the stretching glove. Inconceivably, Clemente was called out, and the fiery ballplayer came very close to striking an umpire. True, Clemente was hitting just .278 at the time, and true, it was a tight ball game, but his anger seems not unusual when one views the photograph. It was clear; Clemente was very, very safe. Except the umpire said he wasn't. They had taken a base hit out of his pocket.

It rankled Clemente. Less than two weeks later, he got into an argument with umpire Bill Jackowski. Clemente pushed Jackowski—"jostled" is the official word—and a few days later he received a wire from league president Warren C. Giles, fining him $250. "Your actions," wrote Giles, in what appears to be a case of overkill, "were the most serious reported to our office in several years." On top of the fine, Giles suspended Clemente five days.

The team could ill afford to lose Clemente. This was 1963, the year Joe L. Brown gambled, and lost. Before the season, Brown traded Dick Groat to St. Louis, Dick Stuart to the Red Sox, and Don Hoak to the Phils. Three-fourths of the infield that had helped win a World Series two seasons ago were gone. In their place, Brown brought up young untested Bob Bailey from the American Association. Bailey had received $150,000 to sign with the Pirates a few years before. Now he was being asked to play third and prove himself in one season. Dick Schofield replaced Groat. Donn Clendenon played first. The gamble failed. Bailey had the jittery freshman season so many bonus youngsters have. He batted .228. Meanwhile, Dick Groat walloped the ball at a .319 clip for the Cardinals, and over in the American League Dick Stuart had a positively super season, belting 42 home runs and leading his league with 118 runs batted in. Dick Schofield, at short for Pittsburgh, hit .246. Young Clendenon batted a not-bad .275, but he was not knocking in runs like Stuart, and he struck out just as often.

There were pitching problems, too. Vernon Law's shoulder got worse. He wound up winning four games in 1963. Law permitted himself to be sent down to the Carolina League, in hopes the southern sun would bake out the soreness. He pitched two complete games in his only starts down there, won them both, and struck out 17 batters in 18 innings, but the batters were not Mays and Aaron. Joe Gibbon won five games and lost twelve.

So the team floundered, and the fans—in total scorn—stayed away in droves. In such an atmosphere nerves are frayed, and men snarl at each other. Clemente and Murtaugh had their run-in.

"The Pittsburgh press," Clemente said to me after the incident, "had me at odds with Danny Murtaugh. One writer always makes propaganda against me. The writers never said exactly I was at odds, but they know how to say it other ways. I caught the flu in San Francisco. Then we flew to Los Angeles, and we had shrimp and steak on the plane. I got sick in my room at three A.M. I began to sweat. I had the shakes. I called the doctor at six. His nurse told me to put hot towels on my stomach. Later that morning, they pumped out my stomach. I went to the ball park. Murtaugh asked me how I felt."

"How do you think I feel?" Clemente answered. "Very bad."

Murtaugh told Bill Mazeroski, team captain, to look over Clemente. Maz asked Clemente how he felt.

"Bad," Clemente said.

"Stick around," Maz said, and went back to Murtaugh, who again approached Clemente.

"Listen," Murtaugh said, "Maz is the captain. He says you can play, so you play."

"Drysdale struck me out twice that day," Clemente recalled. "I had no swing at all. You can imagine." Yet Clemente also had a hit that day.

The next day was a doubleheader in Houston. Clemente spent 40 minutes on the rubbing table, feeling dizzy. Murtaugh tried his own brand of psychology.

"I think you're the best in the league," he told his right fielder. "You make good money. You have to put out."

"I can't play like this," Clemente protested.

Clemente sat out the next three games, which gave the Pittsburgh press a chance to suggest that the star and his manager were not getting along, that Murtaugh was "tired" of Clemente's "attitude."

Clemente understands the implications of all this. He knows what has been said about him, and he resents it. "They think it is an act," he said to me. "When I said I had back trouble, they call me 'Mama's Boy.' 'Goldbrick.' When my elbow was swollen big as a softball, they say it was in my head." It annoys Clemente. It is as though he has been called a liar for protesting that he does not feel well. He does not know that some Americans measure a man's character by his willingness to suffer silently. It is America's Puritan background; we are a repressed people, and we glory in our repression. A man does not complain; he remains a good soldier no matter how much he suffers. All this puzzles Clemente. "If I am sick," he says, "I do not deny. If my back is hurting me and I am forced to punch at the ball, with no power, I tell the truth. I tell them I am hurting."

To Clemente it comes down to truth and falsehood, black and white. Naturally he opts for truth. He has a pain; he admits it.

Yet having said all this, the game is still baseball, not

psychosomatics or philosophy. Clemente was suspended for five days, and he missed a few games during his run-in with Murtaugh, but when the season had ended, he'd played 152 games. Captain Bill Mazeroski played 142 games, yet nobody would ever suggest Maz had dogged it.

For the second season in a row, Clemente had started slowly, hitting .240 after a month of play. But again he warmed up, and by the All Star break he was batting .319. He added to this, and as late as September 17 Clemente led the league in hitting. But despite a four-hit day against the Giants on September 27, and three hits two days later, including a home run on the last day of the season, Clemente batted just .285 the final month, as Tommy Davis caught and passed him. But it was .320, and now Clemente had put together four years in a row over .300—1960, 1961, 1962, and 1963. His career mark topped .300, and for the years of the new decade, no man in baseball had hit as well.

Still, the word is *gloom.* Pittsburgh ended the year 25 games back of pennant-winning Los Angeles, with a 74-and-88 mark. The team had lost 20 more games in 1963 than in 1962. The gamble of dealing off experienced major leaguers for unproved youngsters had failed dismally. The fans showed their displeasure. Now the home attendance was a bare 780,000, down 300,000 from the year before. The team had gone into the red again.

"This past season has been a nightmare to me," Joe L. Brown said.

Yet in this disheartening season, Clemente had come back. He had added eight points to his .312 average, and by now had become a fixture in Forbes Field, a man about whom you built your attack, your team. He had become *the* star, now that Groat was gone. Mazeroski was the captain, and the solid man, but Clemente could do everything, hit, field, run, throw, and do it so elegantly, so excitingly. You could build a defense around and on Mazeroski. You could build a team around Clemente. He had become more than a star, more even than *the* star. He had become the team's key, its pivot.

And for this, Pittsburgh owner John Galbreath had begun to show his generous appreciation. Perhaps not everybody appreciated Clemente. His manager did, and his general manager, and they pay your salary. Clemente's kept increasing. A few years before, he had bought a 1960 Chevrolet Corvair for $2,600, his first big league car. Later, as his salary went up, and his fame, he swapped the Chevy for a $3,000 Pontiac. A ballplayer is an entertainer. He is seen in public, and he can seldom lead a private life. He usually does not care to. He has chosen a public life for somewhat the same reasons an actor chooses a public life, or a politician. He wants the fans' adulation. He begins to want, or need, the trappings of such a life. A Chevy is a good enough car, and so too is a Pontiac, but they are not the glamour cars of public figures.

"Harvey Haddix used to tell me to drive a Cadillac," Clemente once recalled. "Haddix said, 'If you ever drive a Caddy, you will drive nothing else.' "

In 1963 a Pittsburgh car dealer offered Clemente a 1964 Cadillac for $5,400. Two-tone. Avocado green. White top. A star's car. All was not gloom. They say only home-run hitters drive Cadillacs. Fittingly, Clemente's last hit of 1963 was a home run. He drove a Caddy.

12

Batting King: 2

THE 1964 SEASON marked two milestones in Roberto Clemente's life, his tenth year in the big leagues, and his thirtieth birthday, in August.

You could no longer think of him as a boy. He dressed immaculately, and in quiet good taste. He drove his avocado-green, white-topped Cadillac. He earned over $50,-000 in salary, plus a few added dollars in fringe earnings. Not much, but some. Appreciation was not universal, but it had swelled. With it came a stronger sense of confidence. In 1964 Clemente said to a Pittsburgh sportswriter:

"I believe I can hit with anybody in baseball. Maybe I can't hit with the power of a Mays or a Frank Robinson or a Hank Aaron, but I can hit."

The fault lay not wholly in him, Clemente said.

"As long as I hit in Forbes Field, I can't go for home runs. Line drives, yes, but not home runs."

And it was not a one-sided game. You had to field, too.

"I'm a better fielder than anybody you can name. I

have great respect for Mays, but I can get a ball like Willie, and I have a better arm."

In cold print, it reads like conceit. But Clemente never sounds conceited. He speaks softly, with an almost apologetic manner, and when he says he has great respect for Mays, or for anyone, he means exactly that. By 1964, an argument could be made for Clemente's throwing arm as the best in the business.

"I can throw *blind* to a base," Clemente has said, and again it reads like conceit, and sounds like truth. It *is* truth. He has the instinct of the ball-playing genius. Intuitively, he knows where to throw, and he throws it there.

Not that the words are very important. All they mean is that Clemente, in his tenth year, approaching his thirtieth birthday, finally felt enough at home that he could begin to blow his own horn.

In 1964, first Willie Mays, and then Billy Williams threatened to tear the league apart, hit not .350, but .400. But by late July, Clemente had caught both men and put them behind. In August the Pirates came to New York to play the Mets, and in the lobby of the Commodore Hotel, I spoke briefly about the batting race with Pittsburgh's roly-poly catcher, Smokey Burgess.

"Clemente will not be one-two-or-three among the top hitters," Burgess said. "He will be number one. Period."

A year before, Clemente had led this late, but Tommy Davis caught him. This year, nobody was going to catch him. And a second batting title was added to the 1961 crown.

"I beat out Mays, Williams, Aaron," Clemente said, "all those men who are considered ahead of me." It became a source of pride.

In 1964 Clemente batted a strong .339. Nobody in either league hit so high.

Clemente ripped out 211 hits—his career high—and again nobody topped him, though Curt Flood also had 211. Clemente scored 95 runs and batted in 87, for his strongest showing in the power department since 1961. Clemente banged 40 doubles in 1964, another career high, plus seven triples and twelve home runs. He had 301 total bases, more than such acknowledged sluggers as Hank Aaron, Joe Torre, and Jim Hart. But perhaps Clemente was most proud that he played in 155 games. Now nobody could call him a quitter, a man who had not come to play.

Not that it was a totally new Clemente. Early in August in Chicago, on a fearfully hot afternoon, Clemente took his usual stance in the box, with his right foot resting just outside the rear line. The Cub catcher noticed the foot and pointed it out to the umpire.

The umpire told Clemente to get back in the box. The batter's box was redrawn, and a grumbling Clemente bounced out easily to short. Then he removed his helmet and from beyond first base booted it into the Pirate dugout. The crowd booed.

There is a natural grapevine in baseball, and along the vine traveled this latest juicy bit: Get Clemente back in the box. He turns so blind-mad he can't see the ball. So in Philadelphia on August 28, catcher Clay Dalrymple pointed to Clemente's feet and umpire Chris Pelekoudas demonstrated his ability to draw straight lines. Clemente cramped himself into the new box, and promptly singled to right.

Which puts it in perspective. Clemente sometimes wears his emotions on a thin skin. But he is not stupid. He grasped what was happening. In Chicago he had growled at the umpire, "Where you been? I've been batting this way for ten years." But in Philadelphia he kept quiet. His bat spoke.

He won another battle of nerves in 1964. You know by now how Clemente had been the special pigeon of pitcher Bob Purkey. By mid-1964 Clemente had collected ten hits in six years off Purkey, and his career average against the soft pitches of the right-hander was exactly .176. Purkey toyed with Clemente. He threw his nothing ball, slow curves, off-speed pitches, high and outside, low and inside, all over the place except over the plate. Bad balls. Clemente has always feasted on bad balls. But Purkey's were different, and it was famine, not feast. Finally Clemente said to himself, "You win, Purkey." He decided to stop swinging at anything Purkey threw out of the strike zone.

They got together twice in 1964 after the fateful decision, once in Cincinnati and once in Pittsburgh. The first time, Clemente walloped Purkey for three hits. One of them kangarooed over the Reds' center-field fence on one bounce, for a ground-rule double. The next time, in Pittsburgh, Clemente again laid off until Purkey was forced to come in, and again Roberto bombed him for three hits. Six hits in two games, after ten hits in six years.

All this is one way of saying maturity. The years had cut down the idiosyncrasies. He still swung at, and hit, bad pitches, the best bad-ball hitter in his league since Joe Medwick. But when he had to lay off a pitch, he laid off. In 1964 Clemente walked 51 times, more bases on balls than Orlando Cepeda received, or Jim Hart, Joe Torre, or Johnny Callison. No longer was he a wild man at bat.

But to pretend he had totally changed his ways would be incorrect. He still was, to say the least, an unorthodox batter. Listen to Sandy Koufax describe Clemente of 1964:

"Strangest hitter in all baseball. Figure him one way

and he'll kill you another. . . . He's very strong and is extremely quick with his hands. You look at him swinging, sometimes on his front foot, sometimes on his rear, sometimes with both feet off the ground, and you're inclined to think: 'This guy can't hit the ball.' "

But Koufax knew that first inclination could only hurt him. "The longest ball I've ever seen hit to the opposite field was hit off me by Clemente at the Los Angeles Coliseum in 1961. It was a fast ball on the outside corner and he drove it out of the park; not just over the fence, but he knocked it way out. . . . What makes Bob the kind of hitter I don't want to see at bat with runners on is that he's liable to hit anything. He could hit a pitchout for a home run. . . . You can't throw him two of the same pitches in a row. He may look terrible on the first and hit the darnedest shot you'll ever see on the next."

For years Sandy Koufax insisted that Hank Aaron was the best hitter in the league, or at least the toughest for Koufax. Then, in his last season of 1966, Koufax changed his mind. Clemente, he now said, was the most difficult out in the league.

He hit those darned shots all year, the fifth year in a row he would bat over .300, and baseball knew him. The acclaim never did ring for him as it rang for Mickey Mantle or for Willie Mays, but by 1964, by his thirtieth birthday in August, he had secured for himself a place challenged by just a handful. I sat with Clemente the day after his birthday as he sipped iced tea in the Commodore Hotel in New York and talked about his career, and his future.

It was August, and Clemente was tired, as most baseball men are in August. It is the worst month, they will tell you, the heat is terrible, and the fields are baked dry as sand and hard as sandstone. "I don't believe this is the only way to make a schedule," Clemente said that day in August. "I never made a schedule, but I believe I could do as well." And he shook his head.

But what made it difficult was the club's standing. Again Pittsburgh had failed to make a serious charge. The club would wind up tied for sixth and seventh places with the Dodgers. Its record would be 80 wins, 82 losses. Attendance would fall off by another 24,000; only the Cubs and the Houston Colts would draw fewer people. All this discourages a ballplayer and tends to bring bitter memories to the surface. I asked Clemente whether he had any goals for the coming season.

"I have no goals. Have a good season. That is enough. Hitting for average is not the whole thing. My best year was 1960. I should have been voted the Most Valuable Player." Still, he remains a team man, more interested in pennants than in personal tributes. "The year 1961 was good, and so is 1964, but we did not win in 1961, and we are not winning this year. So it is not as good. Winning is fun."

And beyond the next season? How many more did he think lay ahead?

He would play, he said, "another ten years, at full speed." If he needed the money, or if he felt he just had to play some more, "I would go three, four more years, slowed down a little." Baseball, one would judge, was in his blood. When he finally was through, he would coach or manage in Puerto Rico, his home. Yes, he said, they could afford to pay good money to a manager in San Juan.

Of the good money he was earning in 1964, he was sending a portion home. "I have money now," he said. "My folks took care of me when I was young. Now they are old, and I can take care of them." The house he had bought for $12,500 he would now improve, until its worth had doubled.

Clemente cares deeply about his family. When his brother died, Clemente helped pay the expenses of raising the brother's son. The boy moved in with Clemente. Roberto also helped raise the daughter of a sister who had died. Family, in Latin America, is close-knit, loving, protective.

He commented on how Al Dark, then managing the San Francisco Giants, graded his players with pluses and minuses. A plus was given a man who contributed to the total team effort, a minus to a man who may have hit well or fielded well or pitched well, but did not help the team win. Willie Mays received many pluses; Orlando Cepeda, even when he led the league in home runs and runs batted in, was a minus player, according to Dark.

"Terrible," said Clemente. "A manager must never go against his players."

It is not the family way of doing things. A manager is like a parent, and in Clemente's life, he had known only parents who did not go against their children. A man takes his childhood with him into his adult life. These are the ideals a man must have—in Clemente's eyes—or else he is less a man.

But all was not idealistic. A touch of cynicism had entered Clemente, and made him seem more American, more like his Stateside teammates. When he finished his iced tea and his interview, he got up and walked into the hotel lobby. Instantly, youngsters converged on him. He signed their cards until one persistent boy shoved a piece of paper at the star. Clemente, without looking at the youngster, brushed past, head high. "That is his third card," he said. "They sell autographs. They swap them."

Ideals clash with crass reality. It's nice to sign autographs for kids, but not always and not for all kids. In 1955 when Clemente first broke in, he signed autographs over and over, probably never noticing if the same kid came back for seconds and thirds. This new Clemente, of course, is the more sensible one.

Clemente said, of the upcoming winter, "I will not play winter ball. I look forward to a rest. I play too much winter ball in the past. It makes me tired when I go to spring training. Last three winters, I just play half seasons in the Puerto Rican league. Now, no more winter ball. In the spring of 1965, I'll report strong. You see."

He played winter ball.

He hurt himself.

He became very ill.

When spring training began, he was not present.

When he finally reported, he was not strong at all.

He had become entrapped by life, by the grim realities of life, its demands. He had given the word, and he meant it when he gave it, but the word was not so strong, after all. He said he would not play winter ball, but he did, and his career nearly perished.

13

Batting King: 3

THE YEAR seemed to close like most other years of Bob Clemente's baseball life. They held another vote to determine the Most Valuable Player in the National League, and though Clemente had again won the batting title, and had again proved his genius in the field and on the bases, had this time played 155 games, it didn't impress many people.

The baseball writers instead chose Ken Boyer, third baseman for the pennant-winning Cards and the league's leading rbi man in 1964. It was a sound choice. After Boyer came Johnny Callison, a fine right fielder who does everything extremely well, but nothing quite as well as does Clemente. After Callison followed Bill White, Frank Robinson, Joe Torre, Willie Mays, Richie Allen, and Ron Santo. Then—number nine—Roberto Clemente. Clemente had outhit them all, some by more than 40 points. Callison he'd outhit by 65 points.

After the Most Valuable Player poll came the press association all-star teams, and the UPI outfield for 1964 was Willie Mays, Mickey Mantle, and Billy Williams.

But Clemente did not sulk. He had better things to do. Once Clemente had joshed to a fellow Pirate: "It is better to go into the reserves than to marry." It sounds like a bachelor's law, and bachelor's laws tend to be repealed when the right girl wanders onto the scene.

The right girl had wandered. One day Roberto Clemente had gone to the drugstore to pick up medication for one of his many ills. He saw a tall beautiful girl; he learned that her name was Vera Zabala. On November 14, 1964, Clemente married Vera Zabala. Shortly after, he bought a home in Río Piedras, not far from his folks, and he and Vera set up housekeeping.

Meanwhile, Clemente kept busy in other ways. He had been recruited by Puerto Rican District Judge Roberto Morales to help combat juvenile delinquency by setting up baseball clinics on the island. When Roberto was not at the clinics, he made it his business to visit ill children in hospitals. For decades, ballplayers have visited hospitals, bringing cheer to sick kids. Sometimes they also bring photographers, provided by the ball club. It is good publicity.

When Clemente visits the hospital children, he goes alone.

"I do not go because the club wants me to go," he says. "I go because I want to go."

So he kept busy. He also busied himself managing the San Juan club in the Puerto Rican league, which should have been enough, but it wasn't, and by December Clemente had appeared in 15 games. True, he had not played full-time; sometimes he just pinch-hit, or ran, or played a few innings.

It did not make the Pittsburgh front office happy. A

Pirate official said to me, "Naturally we would prefer that Clemente rest. He can't improve any. He does not need to play. They put pressure on him to change his mind. The people in San Juan hounded him until he gave in to the popular demand."

Roberto Clemente has another version. "They want me to play, yes, and I want to help San Juan win the pennant, but I also do it to earn extra money."

Spoken like a true husband.

And like a true husband, Clemente was mowing the lawn of the Río Piedras house on a December afternoon when the blade of the mower struck a stone and propelled it upward against his right thigh with sickening force.

He benched himself, because of the sore leg. Along came the Puerto Rican All Star game, and Clemente was prevailed upon to make a pinch-hitting appearance.

"I could hardly walk," Clemente said. "I couldn't risk running." He batted and hit a typical Clemente shot to right field, and he trotted slowly to first.

Not slowly enough. The leg crumpled. A ligament popped. He felt "something like water draining inside my leg."

Not water. Blood. After the game, he was carried to a car and taken to a doctor.

The leg had started to swell. The next day he couldn't walk. The doctor said it was an internal hemorrhage and gave it three days to stop and drain off. Each day the leg was bigger. Finally the doctor scheduled an operation in a San Juan hospital. The thigh was sliced open and the excess blood drained from the clotted bruise.

A ligament had been torn in the right thigh. By itself, this is not terribly serious. Nearly every sprain involves a torn ligament. Ligaments heal quickly. Still, Clemente was a valuable property, and the alarm by now within the

Pirate organization was large. General manager Joe L. Brown dispatched Caribbean scout Howie Haak, who is equally large, to see Clemente and his doctor. Haak transmitted optimistic reports. But an item in *Sporting News* of February 13, 1965, again cast a dark light on the injury. It quoted Clemente as saying the doctor "told me not to run much in spring training and that it would come around halfway through the season if I took care of it, which I will."

You could see them fainting in the Pirate office. A Clemente partially disabled for half a season is a team deprived of its lone steady gun.

All this, of course, did not have to be. If I may, I should like to suggest a solution to the Pirate front office:

Pay Clemente a salary that represents his worth during the regular season, and then tack onto it a bonus arrangement, not unlike the federal subsidy paid to Stateside farmers if they promise to let their fields lie idle. The soil is replenished, rested. So too would be Clemente rested. The theory is the same, and Clemente's base hits rattling San Juan fences are very likely a crop that could be saved for a Forbes Field harvest. Clemente insists he played winter ball in 1964 because of the money. *Ergo*: pay him *not* to play winter ball.

But all this is water under the dam, or blood under the skin. Clemente had played; he had hurt himself; and the question was whether he'd be able to open the season. Brown, distraught, called Clemente personally, and—according to Jack Berger, Pirate public relations director—Clemente had assured Brown he was well. The reports were exaggerated. He was in good condition. His leg was fine. He'd report for spring training ready to go full speed. Amen.

Not that this must be taken as gospel. Baseball public

relations men are no different from public relations men in other fields. PR men are a peculiar breed. They are born, not made, and you recognize them at birth by their crossed fingers and the hyperbole at their lips. The first word a baseball PR man says is not Mommy or Daddy, but "Phenom." Later, in grade school, when they learn to read, the hyperbole at their lips naturally must be expressed. Thus, it comes out: "See John. See John run. Faster than Cobb."

So I telephoned Clemente in Puerto Rico, and put the same questions. How was he? How was his leg? What shape did he expect to be in when he reported for spring training?

"I feel good," Clemente said, "but my leg is a little weak. I run every day at the beach or the ball park, 15 minutes a day. I told Mr. Brown I was in good shape, and I would be in good shape. He knows I no lie to him. But I will *not* go all-out when I arrive for spring training. Take it slow, easy, at first. I expect to be ready for opening game. Top speed."

This was the middle of February.

The Pirates opened their camp on March 1.

Clemente did not show up.

The Pirates announced that Clemente would be fined $100 for every day he missed.

The next day, out of Puerto Rico, came an announcement from Clemente's doctor, Roberto Buso.

Clemente was in a hospital, with malaria.

He had picked up the malaria germ, apparently, while barnstorming in Santo Domingo. But that was not all. He also was suffering from a systemic paratyphoid infection, transmitted from a hog farm Clemente operates. Malaria, of course, brings on chills and fever, severe shakes and delirium. Paratyphoid's symptoms are fever, nausea, vomiting, and diarrhea. The two, together, obviously had knocked Clemente out.

The first inclination would be to cancel the 1965 season for Roberto Clemente. The mower accident, the torn ligament, the internal hemorrhage, the surgery, the slow convalescence, malaria, and paratyphoid—too much for an army, much less one man. Clemente had always had his share of ailments: leg, back, elbow, stomach, tension headaches. You could not expect such a man—a walking hospital ward—to absorb any new ailments. Especially such critical ones. Cancel him out. Forget 1965.

Clemente finally reported, 15 to 20 pounds underweight (some say 23 pounds), and because Clemente never carries excess weight, you can imagine how skinny he was, weak as a cat. He played a bit in spring training, trying to regain his strength, but he was quite sick, his leg still bothered him, and the aches and pains that have gripped Clemente appeared to have triumphed once and for all. Surely he would not start the season; surely he would not play too much once he did start; surely he could not be expected to compete with healthy athletes, with pitchers who threw baseballs 90 miles an hour.

With Clemente gone, the Pirates had just one solid star. Bill Mazeroski. Mazeroski promptly broke a foot in spring training. He would not play the first month of the season.

But Clemente wasn't gone. Not quite. The season opened. He played. Part-time. Pinch-hitting. Occasional starting jobs. Some running stints. Defensive bits. Not too many of any of these. He missed seven whole games, and the Pirates won two of the seven. But even when he played, the Pirates lost—24 of the first 33 games. The team drifted into last place, a full four and a half games behind the Mets. By May 17 Clemente had come to bat 105 times. He had hit no home runs; he had driven in just nine runs. He was batting .257. By May 21 the club was thirteen and a half games out of first place.

Nor was it only Clemente who'd started weakly. Vernon Law, struggling to overcome the bad shoulder and the rust of inactivity, lost his first five decisions in 1965. Bob Friend was headed for a season of just eight wins.

Clemente began to chafe at his inactivity. True, it was his illness, his injury. But he felt he had recovered sufficiently to play more regularly. He knew he wasn't well (and he did not feel well all season), but he also felt he would get no better on the bench, watching the club move through another dreadful season.

He complained about not playing. The Pirates had a new manager. Danny Murtaugh had gone, the man who had taken a seventh-place club to a pennant and World Series, but had then seen the glory darken as the club drifted downward. He joined Haney and Bragan and all those who had come before. Now it was Harry Walker, an outgoing talkative Southerner who once led the National League in batting, poking hits to the opposite field, truly a singles hitter, but a good one, and a smart baseball man.

But he was new, and a relative stranger, and men need time to get to know each other. So this was a trying time, a testing time, and the Pirates were losing.

One day Clemente reputedly blew a fuse. He wanted to play more regularly, he insisted, and—so the report goes—he didn't want to play for Harry Walker. "I want to be traded. I cannot play for that man," is the way Pittsburgh reporter Al Abrams quoted Clemente. (Later, Clemente denied he'd been that unhappy.)

Clemente—still underweight—began to play regularly. The team began to jell. Mazeroski returned. And the Pirates started to win.

Clemente went off on a hitting tear. Common sense says it could not happen, but it did. Weak as he was, far from ready, he began to hit, and to hit well. He batted safely in 33 of 34 games. True, he still did not have his old power, but there was his average, over .300, over .315, all the way up to .340. The team rose, correspondingly.

From that low point—the first 33 games—the team played superlatively well, winning 20 of the next 22. (The two losses were, incredibly, to the Mets.) Pittsburgh won 81 games and lost 48 in the stretch of the season following that first mediocre month. No team in the league played as well. The pennant-winning Dodgers were 74-and-54 for the same period.

It was too late to win a pennant. A game lost in April cannot be won back in September. The team kept on rushing, charging, winning, but time ran out. They won ten of their last twelve games in 1965, but they ended third, five games back of San Francisco, the Giants another two games behind Los Angeles.

Attendance at Forbes Field also improved, climbing to 909,279, an increase of nearly 200,000 over the previous season. Healthy comebacks flowered all over. The courageous Law, after those first five defeats, won 17 games and lost just four. He won his last nine decisions. Bob Veale, the big left-hander who'd won 18 games in 1964, showed it was no fluke, winning 17 in 1965. In '64 he'd led the league with 250 strikeouts; now he struck out 276 men, and he did it in 266 innings, a Koufax feat. Young Tommie Sisk began to win as a starter, winding up 7-and-3.

And the big new slugger Wilber Stargell, recovering nicely from knee surgery, walloped 27 home runs (three of them in one game against the Dodgers) and drove in 107 runs.

But Clemente's was the greatest comeback. "I never felt 100 percent," he said later, "and I had to keep pushing myself. It was often painful to go up to the plate." Periods of fatigue set in. He could not cope with the full 162-game season. He peaked in mid-August, and then slowly began to sag. He batted .280 from then to the season's end. The Labor Day doubleheader drained whatever strength he still had. He went 0-for-12 in the next three games, fanning eight times. Then he was struck on the elbow by a pitch, and his average fell some more. In eight games, he had just three hits in 29 at bats.

Yet when it was over, the impossible had transpired. Bob Clemente—too sick to report for spring training and too weak to play at anything like his usual pace—managed to hit .329.

Nobody in either league hit as well.

He'd won his third batting title. Only four men in the history of the modern National League had won more than two batting titles. And they are among the finest hitters the league has ever known—Honus Wagner, Rogers Hornsby, Paul Waner, and Stan Musial. Two of them are Pirates—Wagner and Waner. Now there was a third. Roberto Clemente had joined the immortals of Pittsburgh, Wagner and Waner.

Clemente's .329 in 1965 beat out Hank Aaron by 11 points. For a weak man, his 14 triples were second best in the league and his own personal high. He'd missed those seven early days and other days later on, and parts of still more days, but he saw action in 152 games and he collected 194 hits, fourth highest in the league.

You would think—by now, and after this unbelievable year—the trumpets would blow, the fanfare ring.

They shower utility second basemen with gifts and hold a day in their honor if somehow they manage to last four seasons in the league without ever getting caught stealing from the club safe. They vote men the most valuable in their league when they hit .269. Men have been elected to the Hall of Fame with lower averages. And what did they say of Roberto Clemente, sick for the first month and weak all season? They said, "Can you imagine? He's hitting .329, but he's knocked in just 65 runs. The guy's got no power."

Clemente headed for 1966, his reputation now so firmly established it seemed nothing could shake it. Well, perhaps something could shake it—like hitting over 25 home runs, and driving in over 100 runs in one season. That might convince a few doubters. An unlikely occurrence, of course, because Roberto Clemente is a good hitter, *but* he just has no power.

Then came 1966.

14

"If Roberto Doesn't Get It, It Will Be Criminal"

IN 1966 Roberto Clemente became the leader of the Pirates. Not just by deed. He'd led by deed—his flailing bat, his flaming speed, his daring fielding and howitzer-like throwing—for years. Now he led by pronouncement, by existence. Bill Mazeroski remained the captain, and Vernon Law the elder statesman, and each man often spoke for the club.

But when a game was won or lost in 1966, and especially in the frantic days of the stretch run as the Giants, Dodgers, and Pirates clawed at each other in yet another memorable pennant duel, the man the reporters came to see in the clubhouse for the official word was Roberto Clemente.

Baseball leaders tend to be organization men, today. They say what the club wants them to say. They seem to be men out of place in baseball uniforms. They would be more comfortable in charcoal-gray flannel or Italian silk, behind a desk.

Clemente is another kind of leader. He cuts to the core

of the matter. Truth hones his words. Organization men lead because they say meaningless things. It is the mark of the age. Say anything, but for goodness sake, don't say anything. Clemente says little, but he says much.

We have commented on the small changes in Bob Clemente, his slight yielding to the world of compromise. He remained, and remains, truthful. But some of the ways of Statesiders had seeped in. A man cannot live by that too-rigid moral code, by a set of absolutes that permits no compromise. Juan Marichal has the face of a cherub, and for years he acted like one. He hates to throw beanballs. He thinks it is morally wrong, cowardly, dirty, unfair. But in baseball he has been ordered to throw them, and he must throw them, to protect his own teammates. When he does, he becomes a man under terrible stress, a man in turmoil. His world of absolute morality, his too-rigid moral code, cracks badly. You saw it the day he lost total control and beat John Roseboro bloody with his bat. Perhaps had he been less absolute in his morality, had he been less insistent on abiding by a morality that knows no compromise, he might not have cracked so badly.

Roberto Clemente has begun to yield to the sea of gray that fills in the chasm between black and white, between the poles of good and bad.

And it is a change that is also good and bad. Naturally one wants to see ideals held inviolate. So if Clemente slipped from the ideal of absolute right, you could express regret. But it also meant a more sensible approach to life and to baseball. Baseball is not a game for the totally pure in heart. It cannot be, and still be played under fiercely competitive rules. It is hard to win if you love your neighbor, or if you turn every cheek and not strike back. You lose second basemen by the carload that way, permitting enemy runners to come in spikes high, while your own runners slide neatly and politely into the bag and not the baseman. Clemente learned this, and in 1965, for the first time, you could hear him say it.

In September of 1966, the pennant race reached its dramatic climaxes. The Pirates, without adequate starting pitching, lost ground to the Dodgers. The Giants, with a sifting defense, plus an offense that hit home runs but little else, gave up further ground. But the Dodgers could not break free, because Koufax had his aching arm, and their batters were singles hitters. So the three teams staggered into September, and finally, on September 22, in Atlanta, the Braves massacred Pittsburgh, 14–1, and the Pirates fell two games off the pace.

Reporters made their daily trek to the clubhouses, and when they entered the Pirate dressing room, they encountered a furious Bob Clemente.

"The Braves have no respect for our pitchers," he said in anger. "They all come up and dig in. They get toeholds. They've been doing that all year long. Somebody's got to go down in the first inning tomorrow if I have to come in and pitch myself."

He did not have to. Bob Veale pitched, and in the first inning he hit Milwaukee's Ty Cline, and suddenly the Braves loosed their toeholds. Veale shut out Atlanta, 3–0, on four hits, and struck out 12. Nobody had shut out the Braves for two months.

Call it what you will—illegal, against the rules, revenge, dirty. But also call it leadership. No, it is not "nice." You'd think batters could take toeholds at the plate. They call it the batter's box, don't they? But taking such a toehold, digging in at the plate, becomes a mark of disrespect. It seems to say, "We know you pitchers are too chicken to throw tight, too sissified to knock us down." Clemente demanded—for himself, and for his team—respect. He got it.

It did not win the pennant, but then this is not a book of pennant races, though the pennant race is the milieu in which we see Clemente year after year. It is a book on the man and the ballplayer. In 1966 he became a leader. He also became the league's Most Valuable Player, and, we think, the two are related.

When the season started, you had to stretch your imagination to conjure a vision of Clemente, the leader, and Clemente, the MVP. Roberto would be thirty-two years old. On his thirtieth birthday, in August of 1964, he had spoken of ten more years at top speed. But the words might have been an adventure in wishful thinking. Athletes tend to run out of steam well before they are forty. Some are washed up not long after thirty.

With Clemente, one also had to weigh the effects of past illness and injury. Surely they could decimate the man before his expected time. And after his rosy words in 1964 had come the malaria and paratyphoid. You do not throw off, forever, the debilitating inroads of malaria. You can be well one day and stricken with chills, fever, delirium, and uncontrollable shakes the next.

So baseball observers watched, waited, and wondered as Clemente entered the 1966 campaign.

The usual characteristics could be noted. Myron Cope, one of the most literate of all sportswriters, visited Clemente in the off-season and jotted down for readers of *Sports Illustrated* Clemente's description of his bodily ills. He was, at the moment, suffering from splitting headaches, pain in his left heel, a back condition, and insomnia. The back condition was such that Clemente could actually hear a displaced disc in his spine as it jounced back into place every morning during exercises. The sound, Clemente said, went *boop*.

To counter his ills, Clemente had improvised a tonic. Basically, it was a milk shake, but Clemente is not one to restrict himself to mere basics. It had frills and elegance, and probably 3,000 calories. Ice cream, milk, egg yolks, bananas, sometimes pears, sometimes peaches, fruit cocktail, sugar, orange juice, and crushed ice were all thrown willy-nilly into a blender and whirled to a splendid concoction as dense as an umpire's brain. The recipe had a certain insouciance. You put in, Clemente said, as much of any ingredient as you wished.

So one gathered, beneath the bantering of Cope's writing and beyond the litany of complaints, that Clemente actually harbored a healthy body and a sunny spirit.

Before he had finished, Clemente told Cope he saw no reason why he too could not join the power elite, if he wanted to. This too was just a matter of putting into the total picture—the blender—as much of any ingredient as you wished. With Clemente, it was the way his hands gripped the bat. "If I make up my mind I'm going to hit 20 homers this year," he said to Cope, "I bet you any amount of money I can hit 20." It depended, he said, on a minor change in the hands.

Clemente played just two innings of winter-league ball in the off-season. Most of the time he'd spent lolling about his magnificent home in Río Piedras, a house he'd had built for $65,000, now worth considerably more. It was a hilltop split-level house with a glorious view of the bay below, and a 48-foot living room where a $1,000 velvet chair sat on a rich pea-green carpet.

Eventually, of course, Clemente had to leave Río Piedras and his pregnant wife and their tiny son. He reported to Fort Myers to prepare for the 1966 season. It was an optimistic camp. Manager Harry Walker viewed the 1965 third-place finish and drew sustenance from it.

"The way we finished," said Walker, "should show that we can win it if we stay fairly clear of major injuries. I'm proud of this club, because it didn't quit when things were rough. That's the stuff it takes to win pennants."

It takes more stuff, and Walker set out to find it or invent it. He pulled Mateo Alou aside, and told the ex-San Francisco Giant how to improve his hitting. Alou is a compact little man with fine speed, a good eye, and a left-handed swing. In San Francisco, left-handed hitters swung —for the wind blew out to right field, and if you hit a ball to right and got it up in the air, it stood a chance of clearing the wire fence for a home run. But in Forbes Field the wind did not blow very much at all, and the fence was too distant a target for so small a man as Matty Alou.

"Hit the ball to left," Walker advised, as he himself had done in winning a batting title in 1947. Walker had hit exactly one home run that year, but he rapped out 185 other hits, good enough for an average of .363.

Actually, for all the stories about Walker showing Alou how to hit to left and how to bunt, Alou had always known how to do each. With the possible exception of Maury Wills, Alou was probably the best bunter in the league, even before he joined Pittsburgh. And though he tried to accommodate himself to Candlestick's gale wind blowing out to right, he also did some clever poke hitting for San Francisco, aiming for open spaces in left field and left center. Still, Walker did insist Alou give up any notion he might have of breaking Roger Maris's home-run record, and he did insist that Alou more strongly emphasize the art of making contact with the ball. Alou, a pleasant, well-mannered and obedient young man, promised his best.

Walker now turned to Clemente. Almost as if he had never heard the nonsense about Clemente being unable to hit with power, Manager Walker said to his right fielder, "This year I wish you would hit 25 home runs and get 115 runs batted in. We will need it for the pennant."

Had Harry Walker only known how well his wishing well worked (and had he known how much else he needed for that pennant), he might also have said, "Bob Veale, I wish you'd win me 20 games," and to a kid named Woody Fryman, "Woody, let's not poop out after the All Star break."

But he did not. He spoke just to Alou and Clemente.

Fine, said Clemente. He would make an adjustment with his hands, and that would be that.

It was.

It also was a wild and wacky year in Pittsburgh. The year of the Black Maxers, the Green Weenie, the airplane bomb hoax, and the mutiny, the year of two lawsuits, and the emergence of Roberto Clemente, power hitter. It was almost the year of a pennant, but not quite. The Dodgers won, with the Giants a hair behind, and the Pirates two more hairs back of them.

But it was Pittsburgh that provided the main thrills. The club led much of the way, and right until the final weekend, it had a chance to win. But it wasn't only winning that made it a thrill to be at Forbes Field in 1966. There were those Black Maxers, for instance, a parody of the aviation film, *The Blue Max.* Pirate ballplayers dressed themselves in World War I headgear and chalked up absurd signs, and then marched about the clubhouse or posed for photographers.

Then, the Green Weenie. The Green Weenie was just that—a huge plastic frankfurter painted green. Back in the days of 1960, a Pirate trainer had noticed that whenever he pointed a green weenie at the opposition pitcher, Pirate bats came to life. If he pointed it at a Pirate pitcher, it magically produced strikeouts. In 1966 the Green Weenie was recalled and put into mass production. Fans bought them or made them or stole them or found them, or perhaps conjured them into being. And whenever a run was needed or an error to be coaxed from an enemy glove, the Green Weenie was aimed en masse. Naturally, if one GW did its job in 1960, you can imagine the effectiveness of 30,000 GWs. (So why didn't the Pirates beat out the Dodgers? Well, Dodger outfielder Al Ferrara came up with the Mexican Sombrero, a huge hat that somehow warded off the potent effects of the GW. The Dodgers put on MS and effectively neutralized GW. All right, then, how come the Pirates didn't beat out the Giants for second place? The Green Weenie couldn't care less about second place. It was win or nothing.)

So 1966 had something few baseball seasons have anymore. Fun. Baseball, again, became at times a game.

Perhaps it was the atmosphere, as much as the adjustment in his hands, that helped Roberto Clemente to his greatest season. Perhaps the Latin spirit had at last found a home in the States. In other seasons, when a team played as well as the Pirates played all year and then lost out the last week, a fan felt blackhearted, betrayed, tragic. In 1966 a little bit of so-what entered the stadium. Yes, fans lost bitterly and wanted to win prayerfully, but when it didn't work out, you could go home and not snarl at your wife or beat your kids. And the Pirate ballplayers themselves seemed to be saying, when the curtain finally fell and the Giants had swept the last weekend series and the Dodgers had beaten them both out, "All right, you've licked us this year, but watch out. We'll be back."

Our story is not the Pirates of 1966 or of 1967 or any year. It is Roberto Clemente.

In 1966, Clemente did not win his fourth batting title. His average fell off 12 points from 1965 and 22 points from 1964. His final figure of .317 stands 34 points below his 1961 mark, when he first led the league.

So what made this so special a season?

Nearly everything.

Clemente did hit .317, fifth best in the league. But Walker had told Clemente to disregard average. He wanted power. Clemente had promised power.

He delivered it. Clemente belted 29 home runs. Never before had he hit as many as 25. He knocked in 119 runs. Never had he driven in 100. He scored 105 runs. Never had he gone over 100.

For a spell, he led the league in rbi. Finally Hank Aaron passed him. But nobody else.

Clemente had 31 doubles, fifth best in the league. He socked 11 triples, third best. His 342 total bases—far and away a career high—trailed only Felipe Alou's 355. He had 71 extra-base hits, again a career high. Roberto Clemente had at long last joined the power elite. Pitchers walked him intentionally 13 times; they walked Mays intentionally 11 times.

Oh, it was a great year, his greatest. It was the year he got his 2,000th hit, and it was a home run, and it helped win a game. He got his 300th double, and his 100th triple. He started to close in on 1,000 runs scored and 1,000 runs batted in. He put together his seventh year in a row of above .300 batting. Nobody else comes close. He caught Willie Mays in grand-slam home runs, and has passed Roger Maris, Frank Robinson, and Orlando Cepeda.

Everyone knew what a great year it was. But he'd had

great years before. Perhaps not quite as great, but still great enough. Yet never had he seriously been considered the league's Most Valuable Player. This time they considered it. Some went so far as to consider it unthinkable that he not be named most valuable. Jim Murray, the witty Los Angeles sports columnist, said late in 1966, "That he has never won an MVP, of course, is as big a crime as if Spencer Tracy never won an Oscar."

And Manager Harry Walker echoed the words: "If Roberto does not get it, it will be criminal."

He got it. He got it despite the greatest season Sandy Koufax ever had. On November 16, 1966, Clemente was voted the Most Valuable Player in his league by the Baseball Writers of America. He didn't win by much, but then Koufax *had* won 27 games, had posted a mini-e.r.a. of 1.73, had struck out 317 men, had pitched 27 complete games, and had done all this with the agony of an arthritic elbow that threatened to leave his arm permanently crippled. Koufax also won his 27 games supported by a batting attack so tiny as to be invisible.

But Clemente won the award. He collected 218 votes to Koufax's 208. Nobody else was close. Filling out the top ten were Mays, Richie Allen, Felipe Alou, Juan Marichal, Phil Regan, Hank Aaron, Mateo Alou, and Pete Rose.

And perhaps the reason he won is not just all that power hitting. Perhaps it is because, as Manager Walker said, "Clemente is the leader of this club."

From his home in Río Piedras, Clemente said, "It's the highest honor a player can hope for, but I was expecting it. Of course, it could have gone to Koufax, but I had the best season of my career, and I was confident the sportswriters would vote for me. I am thankful they did." And later: "It is something to beat out Koufax. I will treasure this all my life."

He became the first man from his native island to win, and the second Latin. The year before Zoilo Versalles, shortstop for the Twins, had won the American League award. Versalles comes from Cuba.

In winning, Clemente effectively destroyed a last myth: that he does not get along with his manager. It was a whisper heard before—he had not got along with Bragan, with Murtaugh, and now with Walker. Clemente once said to me, and he said it in so offhand a way you could tell he was surprised at the question, "I *always* get along with my manager." In 1966 he proved it. He was asked to throw away a decade of batting technique and adopt a new style. He adopted it, and came close to carrying a ball club to a pennant. He also became one of the great run producers of his league.

Nor did he become a one-sided ballplayer. He threw out 17 men on the bases. Nobody in his league threw out as many, nor anybody in the other league. He played 154 games, testimony again to his newfound stamina and dedication. He began the season with a siege of flu and missed some action, and later in July he became so fatigued he had to sit out a few games, but mainly you could count on Clemente, day after day, to be in the lineup and to produce.

Yet with all, the season had its low spots, for himself and for the team, and with all the joy, there was bitterness as well.

For a spell, the tension of the race so gripped the club it threatened to tear it apart. In mid-July at Forbes Field, with Alvin McBean pitching relief, protecting a 5–3 lead in the ninth inning and two out, Houston's Sonny Jackson beat out a hit. Jim Wynn stepped up, and manager Walker charged out of the Pirate dugout.

"Don't pitch Wynn high," he ordered McBean.

Presto! McBean pitched Wynn high, and Wynn hit it higher, over the fence for a two-run home run.

Enraged now, Walker jerked McBean and put in Billy O'Dell who stopped the Astros. In the bottom of the ninth, the Pirates won. Still, Walker remained angry, and McBean, a man of deep intelligence, said that his manager's words—*Don't pitch high*—had acted as "a negative suggestion."

A few days later, this time in the Astrodome, Wynn came up in the fifth inning, batting against Vernon Law, and again he was served a high pitch, and again he belted it out of sight.

Walker jumped onto the field and briefly chewed out Law, but directed most of his anger at catcher Jesse Gonder.

"How can you call for a pitch like that?" Walker yelled, in full view and hearing of 43,000 fans.

"If you want to call the pitches, go ahead," Gonder replied. The two men shouted some more, and when it came time for the Pirates to take the field in the sixth inning, Walker told Gonder to remain on the bench, replacing him with Jerry May. Fortunately, the Pirates won again, 4–3. But the players may have resented Walker's public dressing down of Gonder and the later rumor that Gonder would be sent to the minors. One player reportedly said, "If Walker sends Gonder out and blames him for the home-run ball, we'll all rebel." Later, Walker cooled off, and he and Gonder shook hands.

But there seemed to be some dissension. Maury Allen, of the New York *Post*, wrote his version of it, and it came out—in the *Post*—that catcher Pagliaroni had punched his manager. Pagliaroni vigorously denied the charge, and filed a suit against the paper and the writer.

Other trouble lay ahead. On July 24 Bob Prince, Pittsburgh radio broadcaster, carrying a tape recorder, walked onto a Delta airlines plane at Dallas, to head for San Francisco. A stewardess asked Prince if she could put the recorder on the luggage rack.

"Oh, no," said Prince glibly, "I'll guard this myself. It's more sensitive than the bomb."

Horrors! He had said the secret word. Bomb! The stewardess hustled into the pilot's cabin, and a few minutes later Prince was politely escorted from the plane, where first Dallas police and then the FBI questioned him. The plane left without Prince who finally showed up in San Francisco at 6 A.M., July 25. He'd gone 26 hours without sleep. Good night, Sweet Prince!

Then there were the usual problems. Bob Veale hurt his back and missed five turns. Gene Alley, the brilliant shortstop, enjoying his finest season, was struck on the head by the Mets' Bob Shaw, and missed four games. Pagliaroni was hitting in the high .280s when he suffered a leg injury and began to tail off, ending at .235.

Plus a decidedly unusual problem. On May 6, after a Friday night game at Philadelphia, Roberto Clemente and his mates dressed and left the clubhouse, headed for the team bus outside Connie Mack Stadium. On the way, fans crowded around the Pirates, asking for autographs. Suddenly there was a brief melee.

"I saw someone coming at me with hands up," Clemente said later, "like he was going to hit me, so I just reached up and pushed him away. I really thought someone was coming to attack. I wouldn't hit anyone without provocation."

But hit somebody he apparently had, or else he pushed

harder than he intended. For nineteen-year-old Bernard Heller had been hurt. He lodged a complaint.

The next morning Clemente was taken to 39th District Police Headquarters for questioning. He was not charged. Detective James Coyle said, "My official report states merely that Clemente admits being in a scuffle."

Clemente now said, "I didn't mean any harm. I'm very sorry." And Walker said, "It's a real shame. The boy's quite a fan." On Wednesday, May 11, an oral surgeon declared he had treated young Heller, who had lost four teeth and suffered a broken jaw. It became a matter of legal action. We will not try to explain the incident. That's up to the courts. But note this. On the evening of the scuffle, the Pirates had scored four runs in the eleventh inning to take a fat 7–3 lead, only to see the Phils storm back with five runs in the bottom of the eleventh to pin a shocking 8–7 loss on Pittsburgh. You cannot lose a game much worse than that. Indeed, it may have been the most bitter loss the Pirates suffered all year. Yes, it was a year of lightheartedness and joy, the Black Maxers and Green Weenies and fun, but there was bitterness, too, and Clemente reacts to bitter defeats bitterly.

But it was not a year of defeats, bitter or otherwise, though the Pirates did not win them all. They won 92 ball games, and Clemente made himself known.

When it was over, the baseball writers looked down the names of 250 ballplayers and said that Roberto Clemente was more valuable to his team than any other man in the league. And before the 1967 season had begun, Clemente's bosses let him know they agreed. Bob Clemente became the first Pirate and one of the few men in all baseball history to sign a contract for $100,000 a year. He stood, now, with Mays and Mantle, Frank Robinson and Aaron.

Appreciation, at last, had come full and sweet to this son of a sugar plantation foreman.

And in return for this appreciation, Roberto Clemente had his greatest year for average, in 1967. He batted .357 and, for the fourth time, won his league's batting championship.

15

"They'll Find Him If He Is Good"

WHEN ROBERTO CLEMENTE joined the Pirates in 1955, not yet twenty-one years old, he became very angry if he struck out. He took out his anger on the plastic helmet a batter wears to the plate.

"After I break 22 helmets," Clemente later related, "Manager Fred Haney, he tells me it will cost me $10 for each one. That's $220, and I do not make so much money then. So I stop breaking hats."

Today Roberto Clemente makes enough money to break all the plastic helmets he wants (and the club would probably turn its head and not notice), but he no longer has to. The furies of youth become channeled to more constructive outlets. Clemente takes it out on pitchers and on baseballs.

But basically he has not changed much from the boy of the island who did not know where Pittsburgh was over a decade ago. He knows where Pittsburgh is, and Chicago and San Francisco and New York, and a hundred towns and cities between America's two coasts. He did not come to baseball as a pioneer from his land, but he came early enough to know he was a stranger, an outsider. Today he has helped change much of the attitude that held him aloof. On the 1966 roster of the major leagues were 50 Latin Americans. In 1967 the number had leaped to 74. Baseball, once merely the national pastime of the people of the United States, is more and more a truly international game. Roberto Clemente helped achieve this change. Bobby Avila and Minnie Minoso had come before him, and others, but Clemente has become one of the most famous of all Latin ballplayers and the most enduring.

Yet little of this has changed him. Image—as Alvin McBean once said—is important to Roberto Clemente. But unlike many other ballplayers, Clemente's image and his real self are nearly identical. He is soft-spoken and gentle, decent and God-fearing, God-loving. He is also a fiery competitor, and he is a man who demands what is his due. Thus he is a man of two contradictory parts—gentle and aggressive, God-fearing and competitive. But so are most of us made up of two parts, aggressiveness and humility. It is another way of saying *human*. Roberto Clemente is human. And he does not pretend to be anything else.

As a ballplayer, what he is is simply the best. George Sisler once said, "Roberto Clemente could be the next .400 hitter."

Danny Murtaugh said, "He hits the ball harder to right field than any right-handed hitter in the game. He's got the best throwing arm of any outfielder in baseball, for both accuracy and velocity."

Jim Davenport said, "Clemente hits nothing but line drives, and a pitcher never knows where to throw the ball to him."

Bill Virdon had said, when he played alongside Clemente, "There's no doubt that Roberto's the best right fielder in baseball. It's phenomenal the way he plays that tricky wall in Forbes Field. He takes ordinary doubles off it and throws the runners out at second. He'll snap throws to first and pick them off when they round the bag wide. He has real strong hands and the best arm in the business."

Mickey Vernon, who twice led the American League in batting, and played with Ted Williams and Joe DiMaggio in their primes, said, "Clemente's the best I've ever seen."

And Joe L. Brown, closest to Clemente over his career, has said, "With his ability, I feel any time he bats under .350 it isn't a good season." Brown echoes Sisler's words: "I think he could be baseball's next .400 hitter."

To which Clemente replies, ".400 is very nice, but I will take .340."

He knows that .340 or even .304 takes a lot of taking. He acknowledges that there are great pitchers in his league, and he knows they will get him out more often than not. He cites Don Drysdale and Juan Marichal as great pitchers, and he remembers a game Cincinnati's Jim Maloney pitched in 1963. "Nobody could see the ball. It was the fastest I ever saw anybody." The pitchers keep getting bigger, stronger, faster, better. On top of this, nobody cares when they put spit on the ball. Hitting has become more difficult each year. General managers may speak wistfully of the next .400 hitter, but in reality they search for the next .300 hitter. In the American League, in 1966, only two men hit .300 or better, Frank Robinson and Tony Oliva.

So Clemente does not have to hit .400 to make his mark. Through all the years of the 1960s—his decade—he has hit better than .300 every year, and better than anybody in the game.

So he may now look back on the game from a position of established excellence, established eminence. What would he advise other youngsters in Latin America, if they too wanted to make their mark in baseball?

"I would say to them, 'Lead a clean life. Be strong. Work hard.' If he is a good player, someone will find him. So many people are looking for ballplayers today. He does not have to look for someone to tell him he is good. They'll find him, if he is good. They'll tell him, if he is good. Don't worry."

With strength, then, and a clean life and hard work—and with talent—perhaps they too can come from the teeming cities and dark-soiled farms of the Caribbean lands. Perhaps they can reach the fame of a Roberto Clemente, a man who is a hero to his people, spoken of—a writer once said—in the same breath as cellist Pablo Casals and Luis Muñoz Marín. Perhaps they can become what Roberto Clemente has become—"a glory to the island."

And a glory to the mainland, as well.

Index

The Author

ARNOLD HANO has been a newspaper writer, book editor, and high school English teacher. Now a full-time writer, he has authored several hundred magazine features, as well as several sports books, including *Sandy Koufax: Strikeout King* and *Greatest Giants of Them All*. Mr. Hano lives in Laguna Beach, California.